CISTERCIAN
CHRONICLES AND NECROLOGIES

Previously published by Gracewing

The Cistercians in the Early Middle Ages
The Welsh Cistercians
The Five Wounds of Jesus
The Tudor Cistercians

CISTERCIAN CHRONICLES AND NECROLOGIES

DAVID H. WILLIAMS

GRACEWING

First published in England in 2022
by
Gracewing
2 Southern Avenue
Leominster
Herefordshire HR6 0QF
United Kingdom
www.gracewing.co.uk

All rights reserved

No part of this publication may be reproduced, stored in a retrieval system, or transmitted in any form or by any means, electronic, mechanical, photocopying, recording or otherwise, without the written permission of the publisher.

© 2022, David H. Williams

The right of David H. Williams to be identified as the author of this work has been asserted in accordance with the Copyright, Designs and Patents Act 1988.

The cover image shows the title page of the necrology of Baudeloo (Ghent University Library, BHSL.HS.0481). Reproduced by permission of Ghent University Library, CC-BY-SA.

ISBN 978 085244 983 7

Cover design by Bernardita Peña Hurtado
Typeset by Word and Page, Chester, UK

Contents

Foreword and Acknowledgements	vii
Abbreviations	xi
A. Cistercian Chronicles and the Events of Nature	1
B. Cistercian Necrologies	29

NECROLOGE
DE L'ABBAÏE
DE NÔTRE-DAME
DE PORT-ROÏAL
DES CHAMPS,
ORDRE DE CÎTEAUX,
INSTITUT DU SAINT SACREMENT,

QUI CONTIENT

LES ELOGES HISTORIQUES AVEC LES EPITAPHES des Fondateurs & Bienfaiteurs de ce Monaftére, & des autres perfonnes de diftinction, qui l'ont obligé par leurs fervices, honoré d'une affection particuliére, illuftré par la profeffion Monaftique, édifié par leur pénitence & leur piété, fanctifié par leur mort, ou par leur fépulture.

Ecce ego & pueri mei, quos dedit mihi Dominus in fignum, & in portentum Ifraël à Domino exercituum, qui habitat in monte Sion. Ifaï. VIII. 18.

Me voici moi & les enfans que Dieu m'a donnez, pour être par l'ordre du Seigneur des armées, qui habite fur la montagne de Sion, un prodige & un figne miraculeux dans Ifraël.

Beati mortui qui in domino moriuntur.

A AMSTERDAM,
Chez NICOLAS POTGIETER, Libraire, vis-à-vis la Bourfe. 1723.

Foreword & Acknowledgements

Studying at Cambridge in the mid-1950s, in my final year in the Faculty of Geography, I specialised in historical geography, hence the character of the first section of this volume. I owed my place at Trinity to Mr Vaughan Lewis, one of the few geography Fellows of that college, and my studies in historical geography to the inspiring lectures of, and excursions led by, Miss Jean Mitchell, as well as the course of lectures delivered by Harriet Wanklyn (Mrs Steers) on central Europe. Much of my life has been devoted to the study of Cistercian history, and to visiting Cistercian monasteries, past and present, throughout Europe and the Near East, and I consider this book in many ways a supplement to that published in 1998.

Along the way I have been much helped by monks of the Order, not least the late Fr Edmund Mikkers, OCSO, who in the journal *Cîteaux* published a number of my early articles. On my travels several other religious have allowed me to study in their libraries, and have accompanied me to remote sites. I must mention especially Abbot Benedykt Matejkiewicza, O.Cist., President of the Polish congregation, and abbot of Wąchock; Prior Aleksy Chalcarz, O.Cist., of Jędrzejów, and Father Ferenc Hervay, O.Cist. of Zirc, all now departed, but who welcomed me even though their countries at the time had Communist régimes, and my presence might have drawn unwelcome attention to their monasteries.

Particularly as relates to Part B of this work, I am extremely grateful to all those scholars, archivists and librarians, who have provided photocopies of articles and manuscripts, led me to other bibliographical sources, given translations, or in other ways have assisted my researches. In these respects I offer my sincere thanks, in alphabetical order, to: Wilma Buchinger and Ingeborg Forman of the National Library of Austria; Riccardo Cataldi, librarian of the monastery of Casamari; Emmanuel Cheron of Colmar Municipal Library; Professor Matthew Driscoll of the University of Copenhagen; Johannes Fahlström of the National Library of Sweden; Emmanuel Federbe of Mediathèque Simone Veil, Valenciennes; Katharina Fischer of the Staatsbibliothek, Berlin; Brother Nivard Halász of Zirc Abbey; Father Konrad Ludwig, of Neuzelle Priory; Frère Michel of Hauterive Abbey; Dr Andrzej Nienartowich of Toruń University; Dr Irene Rabi, Lilienfeld Abbey Archives and Library; Mrs Fran Stroorbart of the Royal Library of Belgium, and Jelle Tromp of the National Library of Holland. My sincere apologies to anyone whose name I may have inadvertently omitted. I must draw attention to a fine relevant volume: Piotr Oliński, *Cysterskie nekrologi na Pomorzu Gdańskim od XIII do XVII wieku*, Toruń, 1997.

Numerous scholars and monks have assisted me in the preparation of this volume, and their names are acknowledged later in the text. Lastly, but far

Foreword & Acknowledgements

from least, I express my thanks once again to Mr Tom Longford, and Gracewing, for the pleasing appearace both of this book, and my previous works.

David H. Williams
College of St Barnabas,
Lingfield, Surrey

Abbreviations

A: Austria, B: Belgium, C: Czechoslovakia, D: Denmark, E: England, F: France, G: Germany, H: Holland, Hg: Hungary, I: Italy, L: Latvia, P: Poland, S: Scotland, Sw: Switzerland, W: Wales.

AA — *Annales de l'abbaye d'Aiguebelle*, ed. a monk of the monastery, Valence, 1863.
AC — *Annales et Notae Colbaczienses*, ed. W. Arndt, in *MGH* XIX. Arndt.
ACC — *Annales Ceccanenses*, ed. G. H. Pertz, in *MGH* XIX, 1866 (this work is the same as the chronicle of Fossanova, listed below).
ACK — 'Extracts from the Annals of Crokesden Abbey', ed. F. F. Madden, in *Collectanea Topographica et Genealogica* II, London, 1835.
AH — *Annales Cisterciensium in Heinrichow*, ed. W. Arndt, in *MGH* XIX, 1866.
AL — *Annales Lubenses*, in *MGH* IX, 1851.
ALY — *Chronique de l'Abbaye de Notre-Dame de Longuay*, ed. E. Collot, Paris/Langres, 1868.
AM — *Annales de Margam*, in *Annales Monastici* I, ed. H. R. Luared, London, 1864.
AO — *Annales Olivensis*, ed. W. Kętrzyński, in *MPH* VI, 1893.
AU — *Auctarium Ursicampinum*, in *MGH* IX, 1851.
AW — *Annales Monasterii de Waverleia*, ed. H. R. Luard, in *Annales Monastica* II, London, 1865.
AZ — *Annales Zwetlenses*, ed. G. H. Pertz, in *MGH* IX, 1851.
CA — *De kroniek von het klooster Aduard*, ed. H. Brugmans, in *Bijdragen en meddeelingen van het Historisch Genootschap* 23, 1902.
CF — *Cronaca de Fossa Nova*, in *Cronisti e scrittori sincroni Napoletani* I, Naples, 1845.
CK — *Die Chronik des Klosters Kaisheim*, ed. F. Hüttner, Tübingen, 1902.
CKS — *Chronik des Klosters Stams*, ed. C. Haidacher, Innsbruck, 2000.
CLP — *The Chronicle of Louth Park Abbey*, ed. E. Venables, tr. A. R. Maddison, Linolnshire Record Society, 1891.

Cistercian Chronicles and Necrologies

CM   *Chronica de Mailros*, ed. J. Stevenson, Edinburgh, 1835.

CMC   *Chronicon Monasterii Campensis*, ed. H. Keussen, in *Annalen das Historichen Vereins für den Niederrhein* III, Cologne, 1869.

CMM   *Chronica Monasterii de Melsa* I, ed. E. A. Bond, London, 1866; III, 1867.

CO   *Chronicon Olivensis*, ed. Abbot Stanislas, in *MPH* VI, 1893.

CMN   *Chronicon Manniae et Insularum*, ed. P. A. Munch and A. Goss, Manx Society 22–3, Douglas, 1874. (Probably written by a monk of Rushen Abbey in 1261–2.)

CP   *Chronicon Portense*, ed. I. Pertuchi, Leipzig, 1612.

CR   *Chronicon Riddagshusense*, ed. G. Zimmermann, Brunswick, 1983.

CS   *Chronik des Klosters Schöntal*, ed. O. J. H. Schönbut, Mergentheim, 1850.

CTD   *Chronique de l'abbaye de Ter Doest*, ed. F. V. and C. G., Bruges, 1845.

CTM   *Chronicon Monasterii Claratumbensis*, ed. Q. Kętrzyński, in *MPH* VI, 1893.

CW   *Chronicon Waldsassen*, ed. A. F. Oefelius, in *Rerum Boicarum Scriptores* I, 1763.

CWK   *Chronicon Walkenredens*, ed. M. H. Eckstorm, Helmstedt, 1617.

CZ   *Kronika Zbraslavská* [Chronicon Aulae Regiae], Petra Žitavského [Peter of Zittau], ed. J. Emler, in *Fontes Rerum Bohemicarum* IV, Prague, 1884.

FHT   *Flores Historiarum* III, ed. H. R. Luard, London, 1890 (pages 328–48 very probably derived from Tintern Abbey, Wales).

MA   *Monasticon Anglicanum* V, ed. W. Dugdale, London, 1825

MGH   *Monumenta Germaniae Historica Scriptorum*, ed. G. H. Pertz.

MPH   *Monumenta Poloniae Historica*

NA   *Necrologia Aldersbacensia*, in *NG* IV, ed. M. Fastlinger, Berlin, 1920.

NAL   *Necrologium Altenburgense*, in *NG* V, ed. A. F. Fvchs, Berlin, 1913.

NAP   *Obituaire de l'abbaye d'Aulps en Chablais*, ed. P. A. Naz, in *Mémoires et documents publiés par la Société Savoisienne d'Histoire et d'Archéologique* XV, 1875.

NAR   *Obituaire de l'abbaye d'Argenton de l'Ordre de Cîteaux*, ed. V. Barbier, in *Analectes pour servir à l'histoire ecclésiastique de Belgique* XXXII, 1906.

NAV   *L'Abbaye de l'Arrivour*, in *Recueil des historiens de la France: Obituaires* IV, Paris/Lille, 1923.

Abbreviations

NAZ Necrology of Altzelle, online, at *Fragmentarium: Altzelle: Reconstructio Fragmentarium, University of Fribourg, Switzerland*, lat 183, lat. 208, MS 38.
NB Obituarium van de Baudelo Abdij, in *Liber Beate Marie de Bodelo*, Gand [Ghent], 1586, ed. J. Hoorenbaut, Ghent University Library MS 481 (ff. 2–46), now online.
NBE 'Die zisterzienserabtei Bebenhausen', ed. J. Sydow, *Germania Sacra*, N.F. 16, 1984.
NBH 'Kalendar und Necrolog des Klosters Billigheim', ed. K.-H. Mistele, *Cistercienser-Chronik* 69, N.F. 61/62 (December 1962).
NBL: Abbaye de Boulancourt, in *Recueil des historiens de la France: Obituaires* IV, Paris/Lille, 1923.
NBM Obituarium Monasterii Loci Sancti Bernardi, 1237–1900 (Bornem), ed. B. van Doninck, Lierre, Antwerp, 1900.
NBN 'Nécrologe de l'abbaye de Boneffe', ed. J. Defex, in *Analectes pour servir à l'histoire ecclésiastique de Belgique* VII, 1870.
NBR 'Liber Mortuorum Brunnbacensis renovatus anno 1585', ed. J. von Kühles, *Archiv des Historischen Vereins von Unterfranken und Aschaffenburg* 21, 1871.
NBT Das Totenbuch des Cistercienserfrauenklosters Baindt, ed. L. Walter, O.Cist., in *Württembergische Vierteljahrshefte für Landesgeschichte*, n.s. 26, Stuttgart, 1917.
NC Le Nécrologie de Cambron, in *Annales du Cercle Archéologique de Mons* XVII, 1884.
NCD Abbaye de La Cœur-Dieu, in *Recueil des historiens de la France: Obituaires* III, 1909.
NCR 'Abbey of Croxden', in *MA*.
NDP Necrology of Notre-Dame-des-Prés, MS 0838, Médiathèque Simone Veil, Valenciennes.
NE Necrologium Monasterii Engelscellensis, ed. M. Fastlinger, in *NG* IV, Berlin, 1920.
NEB Brevia Notitia Monasterii B.V.M. Ebracensis, Rome, 1739.
NEBR Series Abbatum et Religiosorum Exempti Monasterii Ebracensis, ed. J. Jæger, in *Cistercienser-Chronik* 14, 1902.
NF Necrologium Fuerstencellense, in *NG* IV, ed. M. Fastlinger, Berlin, 1920.
NFD 'Necrologium Feldbacense', ed. F. L. Baumann, in *NG* I, Berlin, 1888.
NFN 'Necrologium Fürstenfeldensis', ed. F. L. Baumann, in *NG* III, Berlin, 1905.

Cistercian Chronicles and Necrologies

NFR 'Necrologium Frauenthalense', ed. F. L. Baumann, in *NG* I, Berlin, 1888.
NFRW 'Cistercienserinnen-Kloster Frauenthal' (in Württemberg), *Cistercienser-Chronik* 17, no. 192, February 1905 (with a necrological listing).
NG *Necrologia Germaniae*
NGn 'Gnadenthal', *Cistercienser-Chronik* 18, no. 207; May, 1906.
NH 'Monumenta Necrologica Monasterii Sw. Crucis' (Heiligenkreuz), ed. A. F. Fvchs, in *NG* V, Berlin, 1913.
NHB 'Nekrologium des Klosters Heilsbronn aus dem 13–14 Jahrhunderts', ed. Dr Kerler, *Jahresbericht des Historischen Vereins von Mittelfranken* 33, 1865.
NHG Unpublished necrologies of certain Hungarian abbeys.
NHK *Fragmenten van een martyrologium uit de addij Herkenrode*, ed. B. Uijttewaal, 2013 (online).
NHN 'Necrolog des Stiftes Hohenfurt', ed. Sw. Kühweg, in *Urkundenbuch zu Hohenfurt*, Vienna, 1865.
NHR *Nécrologie de l'abbaye cistercienne d'Hautrive*, Bernard de Vevey, Berne, 1957 (manuscript).
NJ *Abbaye des Jardins, près Pleurs*, in *Recueil des historiens de la France: Obituaires* IV, Paris/Lille, 1923.
NJD *Liber Mortuarum Monasterii Andreoviensis*, ed. W. Kętrzyński, in *MPH* V, Łwów, 1888.
NK 'Necrolog des Klosters Kołbacz', ed. R. Prümers, in *Pommersches Urkundenbuch* I, Stettin, 1877.
NKH 'Liber Anniversorium et Necrologium Monasterii Kaisheimensis', F. L. Baumann, in *NG* I, Berlin, 1888.
NKM *Liber Mortuorum Monasterii Camenecensi*, ed. H. de Smalkald, Wrocław University Library, microfilm online, IV F 216.
NKN *Liber Mortuorum Monasterii Coronoviensis*, ed. A. Mańkowski, Fontes Towarzystwo Naukowe w Toruniu XXV, 1931.
NL *Das Todtenbuch des Cistercienser-Stiftes Lilienfeld*, ed. H. R. von Zeissberg, Vienna, 1879.
NLA *Liber Mortuorum Monasterii Landensis*, ed. W. Kętrzyński, *MPH* V, Łwów, 1888.
NLC *Epitome Fastorum Lucellensium*, ed. B. Buchinger, Basle, 1667.
NLD 'Monumenta Necrologia Campi Liliorum', ed. A. F. Fvchs, in *NG* V, Berlin, 1913.
NLH 'Nekrologische Notizen aus Kloster Langheim', ed. Tezelin Halusa, *Cistercienser Chronik* 19, no. 224, 1907.

Abbreviations

NM Abbaye de Maubuisson, in *Recueil des historiens de la France: Obituaires* I, part 2, Paris/Lille, 1902.
NMD Nécrologe de l'abbaye de Marche-les-Dames, in *Analectes pour servir à l'histoire ecclésiastique de Belgique* VIII, 1871.
NML 'Excerpta e Libris Mortuorum Monasterii Mogilensis', ed. W. Kętrzyński, in *MPH* V, Łwów, 1888.
NMS Obituaire de l'abbaye de Moulins, in *Analectes pour servir à l'histoire ecclésiastique de Belgique* XXXIII, 1907.
NN Todtenbuch des Klosters Neuencamp, ed. R. Prümers, in *Pommersches Urkundenbuch* I, Abt. 2, Stettin, 1877.
NNB 'Beiträge zur Geschichte des auf gehohenen Cister-Stiftes Neuberg', ed. P. Lindner, OSB, *Cistercienser-Chronik* 16, no. 180, 1904.
NNC *Necrologium Novacellense*, kindly provided by Fr Konrad Ludwig, O.Cist.
NNH 'Abbey of Newenham', in *MA*.
NNM 'Abbey of Newminster', in *MA*.
NO Nécrologie de l'abbaye de Orval, in *Analectes pour servir à l'histoire ecclésiastique de Belgique* III, 1866
NOL Liber Mortuorum Monasterii Beatae Mariae de Oliva, ed. W. Kętrzyński, in *MPH* V, Łwów, 1888.
NOL1–3 'Die Mönch von Oliva', ed. A. Lubomski, *Cistercienser-Chronik* 51 (1939), 52 (1940), 53 (1941).
NP Abbaye de Preuilly, in *Recueil des historiens de la France: Obituaires* I, part 2, Paris/Lille, 1902.
NPL Liber Mortuorum Monasterii Pelplinensis, ed. W. Kętrzyński, in *MPH* IV, Łwów, 1884.
NPR Abbaye de Port Royal, in *Recueil des historiens de la France: Obituaires* I, part 2, Paris/Lille, 1902.
NPRL Necroloqe de l'abbaïe de Nôtre Dame de Port Roïal des Champs, Amsterdam, 1723.
NPRL2 Supplement au Nécroloqe de l'abbaïe de Notre-Dame de Port-Royal des Champs, 1735.
NPS Das Nekrolog der Cisterzienser-Abtei Pairis, ed. J. B. M. Clauss, *Mitteilungen der Gesellschaft für Erhaltung der Geschichte Denkmaler im Elsass* 22, 1908.
NPS1 Necrologium Parisiense, in J. Rathberger, *Die Herrschaft Rappelstein*, Strasbourg, 1874.
NR Monumenta Necrologica Raitenhaslacensia, ed. Sw. Herzberg-Fränkel, in *NG* II, Berlin, 1904.
NRE Necrologium Runense (Rein), ed. Sw. Herzberg-Fränkel, in *NG* II, Berlin, 1904.

xv

Cistercian Chronicles and Necrologies

NRL   Abbaye de Reclus, in *Recueil des historiens de la France: Obituaires* IV, Paris/Lille, 1923.
NRM   *Het Necrologium der Adellijke Abdij van O. L. Vrouw Munster te Roermond*, ed. J. B. Sivré, Roermond, 1876.
NRN   Excerpta ex Necrologio Antiquissimi Monasterii Runensis, in *Diplomataria Sacra Ducatus Styriae* II, ed. J. F. C. Christian, Vienna, 1756.
NS   R. Kalcher (ed.), 'Die Urkunden des Klosters Seligenthal', *Verhandlung des Historischen Vereins für Niederbayern* 29, 1893; 33, 1897.
NSA   Necrologium Saeldentalense, in *NG* IV, 1920.
NSB   A. Carolei, 'Il martirologio della Certosa di Santo Stefano', L. M. Cerasoli, *Archivio storico per la Calabria e la Lucania* XII, 1942.
NSC   'Die Cistercienser-Abtei Schönau', ed. M. Wieland, *Cistercienser-Chronik* 19, no. 218, April 1907.
NSL   'Das Totenbuch der Abtei Salem', ed. L. Walter, *Cistercenser Chronik* 40, no. 467, 1928.
NSLB British Library, London, Add. MS 18495 (Val St Lambert, B).
NSN   'Kloster Sonnenfeld', *Cistercienser Chronik* 13, no. 153, Nov. 1901.
NSO   'Obituaire de l'abbaye de Soleilmont', *Documents et rapports de la Société Paléontologique et Archéologique de l'Arrondissement Judicaire de Charleroi* 19, 1893.
NSR   *Necrologium Monasterii Loco Dei in Sora 1518*, ed. J. Langebek, *Scriptores Rerum Danicarum Medii Aevi*, Copenhagen, 1776.
NSS   'Een Necrologium der St. Servaas-abdij te Utrecht, *Archief voor de geschiedenis van het aartisbisdom Utrecht: bijdragen* 27, 1901.
NST   *Necrologium Stamsense*, F. L. Baumann, in *NG* III, Berlin, 1905.
NSU   'Biographische Notizen', in 'Beitrage zur Geschichte des Klosters St Urban', *Cistercienser-Chronik* 10, no. 117, Nov. 1898.
NT   *Necrologium Tennenbacense*, ed. F. L. Baumann, in *NG* I, Berlin, 1888.
NTK   *Necrologium Tennikonense* (Lilienthal), ed. F. L. Baumann, in *NG* I, Berlin, 1888.
NTN   'Abbey of Tintern', in *MA*.
NV   *Nécrologe de l'abbaye de Villers, 1574–1792*, in *Analectes pour servir à l'histoire ecclésiastique de Belgique* IX, 1872.

Abbreviations

NVA   *Abbaye du Val*, in *Recueil des historiens de la France: Obituaires* I, part 1, 1902.
NVL   *Abbaye de Vauluisant*, in *Recueil des historiens de la France: Obituaires* I, part 1, 1902.
NW   *Die ältesten Todtenbücher des Cistercienser-Stiftes Wilhering*, ed. O. Grillnberger, Graz, 1896.
NWL   *Necrologia Wilheringensis*, in *NG* IV, Berlin, 1920
NWD   *Necrologium Waldense*, in *NG* I, Berlin, 1888.
NWN   Johannis de Trokelowe, *Annales Edwardii II*, Oxford, 1729.
NWT   *Necrologium Wettingense*, ed. F. L. Baumann, in *NG* I, Berlin, 1888.
NWV   'Zur Geschichte der Abtei Waverley', *Cistercienser-Chronik*, 18, no. 206, April, 1906.
NZ   *Annales Necrologici in Calendario Zwettlensi*, ed. A. F. Fvchs, in *NG* V, Berlin, 1913.
RCC   *Radulphi de Coggeshall Chronicon Anglicanum*, ed. J. Stevenson, London, 1875.
RCH   *Rocznik cystersów henrykowskich*, ed. A. Bielowski, in *MPH* III, Łwów, 1878.
SWW   *The Cistercian Abbey of Strata Florida*, Stephen W. Williams, London, 1889.

✛ PART A ✛

CISTERCIAN CHRONICLES AND THE EVENTS OF NATURE

An essay in historical geography

INTRODUCTION

Two deeply researched articles by L. G. D. Baker examine 'the Genesis of English Cistercian Chronicles', referring mostly to the foundation history of Fountains abbey in Yorkshire.[1] In Wales, Julian Harrison has examined the background to 'the Tintern Abbey Chronicles',[2] and has also contributed a chapter entitled 'Cistercian Chronology in the British Isles'.[3] I wrote an account of Cistercian chronicles some twenty years ago,[4] and the purpose of my present article is to determine in greater detail the information the chronicles give of physical events which affected everyday life: climatology and tectonics.

Cistercian chronicles have much to say in the field of natural history. Set against the year 1186, the chronicler of Schöntal (G) told how 'In January trees blossom, in February the fruits grow, in May the crop has come, and in August is the harvest of fruit and wine in abundance'.[5] When, in 1192, monks from Waldsassen (G) founded a monastery at Osek in Bohemia, its chronicler thought that their going

---

[1] L. G. D. Baker, 'The Genesis of English Cistercian Chronicles', *Analecta Cisterciensia* 25, 1969, pp. 14–41, and 31, 1931, pp. 179–212.
[2] In *The Monmouthshire Antiquary* 16, 2001, pp. 84–98.
[3] In *The Chronicle of Melrose Abbey: A Stratigraphic Edition*, Scottish History Society, 2007, pp. 13–28.
[4] David H. Williams, *The Cistercians in the Early Midde Ages*, Leominster, 1998, pp. 106–7.
[5] *CS*, p. 23.

there would be 'as fruitful to that region as the Nile irrigating the lands adjacent to it in Egypt'.[6] Alas, more often the information the chronicles convey is far from positive. As Joseph Stevenson commented, when editing the chronicle of Coggeshall (E), it told of 'floods, frosts and tempests, of thunder and lightning, together with the famines and pestilences by which they were followed'.[7]

The date on which various events occurred is frequently precisely stated, and thereby reflects the religious background of a nation. The chronicle of Louth Park (E) records a great flood in 1253 as taking place 'on Friday the morrow of the feast of S Dionysius', in other words on 10 October that year.[8] The Coggeshall (E) chronicle, describing a 'marvellous sign in the sky' in 1104, tells of its happening on 'the 7th of the Ides of June, in the week of Pentecost', namely 7 June that year.[9]

The same event may appear in the narrative of more than one chronicle, with occasionally a slip in the date of the year concerned. The chronicle of Mann (written at Rushen Abbey (E)), and the chronicles of Coggeshall (E) and Louth Park (E), all record an eclipse of the sun on 2 August 1133.[10] The annals of Margam (W) and the chronicle of Coggeshall (E) both

[6] CW, p. 57.
[7] RCC, p. xv.
[8] CLP, p. 16.
[9] RCC, p. 5.
[10] CMN, online, non-paginated; RCC, p. 9; CLP, p. 4 (where 1134), respectively.

tell, in precisely the same wording, of two comets appearing on 2 October 1097, 'the larger moving eastwards, the smaller towards the south'.[11] The annals of Zwettl (A) and the chronicle of Oliwa (P) both tell of a massive earthquake in Corinthia and elsewhere, 'on the feast of the Conversion of St Paul' (25 January) in 1348.[12]

A great deal of other information appears in the chronicles: the foundation and building histories of the monasteries—the chronicle of Stams (A) is noteworthy in this respect—as well as the succession of abbots, and other internal monastic matters. Local, national and international affairs may appear, perhaps gained from travellers staying as guests. We also learn occasionally of a change in coinage in the country concerned. I was pleased to note that the chronicle of Aduard (E) records the construction there in about 1270 of 'the laver where monks wash their hands before going to the altar or the table', something I have seen a number of times.[13]

THE SKIES

The Wise Men came to Jerusalem saying 'we have seen a star in the east' (Matthew 3: 2), and Our Lord said to the Pharisees, 'You know how to interpret the

---

[11] *AM*, p. 6; *RCC*, pp. 3–4, respectively.
[12] *AZ*, p. 684; *CO*, pp. 342–3, respectively.
[13] *CA*, p. 49.

appearance of earth and sky' (Luke 12: 56), but also quoted sayings of His time: 'You say in the morning, it will be stormy today, for the sky is red and threatening' (Matthew 16: 3). Throughout history unusual happenings in the sky have made people concerned. The chronicler of Louth Park (E) recorded against the year 1177 that on Sexagesima Sunday (27 February that year), 'A dreadful redness was seen in the sky, like as at mid-summer'.[14]

In perhaps 1317, an undated chronicle entry very probably penned by a monk of Tintern (W), related that on the Monday after Trinity Sunday (29 May that year), 'The sun appeared, blood-red in colour, a sign of the battle in the Holy Land'.[15] The chronicle of Coggeshall (E) relates that in 1194, on the Nativity of St John the Baptist (24 June), there appeared in the sky 'two circles, one large, one small, which fateful sign lasted from the hour of Terce to the hour of Sext; the inequality of the circles suggests a tempest to follow'.[16] On the feast of St Boniface, 5 June 1192, the abbey of Aduard (H) was founded, its chronicler noting that 'The many illuminations of the night presaged a firm belief for its future'.[17]

The chronicle of Melrose (S) related that in 765, 'the sun's rays were seen to be on fire', and that in 793, 'there were seen in the air flaming dragons, a sign

[14] CLP, p. 8.
[15] FHT, p. 341.
[16] RCC, pp. 65–6
[17] CA, p. 36.

Comets

of the two plagues which followed'.[18] The chronicle of Meaux (E) told how, in 1189, the sign of the Cross appeared in the sky above Dunstable in Bedfordshire.[19] The annals of Waverley (E) relate how, on 20 February 1246, in Cheshire, 'large, wondrous red balls fell from the clouds to the ground'.[20]

COMETS

The *Oxford English Dictionary* defines a comet as 'a nucleus of ice and dust which, when near the sun, has a diffuse tail, and typically follows a highly eccentric orbit around the sun'. The compiler of the chronicle of Melrose (S) was less certain, for he wrote: 'A comet is a star which is not (in being) at all times, but appears mostly on the death of a king, or the defeat of a country'. This entry was assigned to the year 1164, noting the appearance 'before the beginning of August of two comets, one to the south, the other to the north'.[21] The passage was copied into the Chronicle of Mann (E).[22]

Comets made intermittent appearances, thus being more notable and more fearful when they did arrive. The chronicle of Fossa Nova (I) told how on 3 June

---

[18] *CM*, pp. 7, 11, respectively.
[19] *CMM* 1, p. 247.
[20] *AW*, p. 338: 'large meteoric stones' is one interpetation.
[21] *CM*, p. 79.
[22] *CMN*, online: where the word *religionis* wrongly replaces *regionis*.

1098, 'a comet appeared, the sky was on fire, and the sun obscured', and how in 1108 there appeared in Italy 'for forty days, a star with a tail'.[23] The chronicler of Coggeshall (E), referring to an event in perhaps 1199, told of the appearance of a comet for fifteen days in November, 'prefiguring the horrible thunderstorms heard on the morrow of St Thomas the apostle'.[24]

Comets were indeed seen as heralds of bad tidings. Of 1316, the chronicler of Zbraslav (C) noted that a comet appeared from the north, 'from the feast of St Andrew [30 November] to that of St Matthias [24 February]', and wrote, in retrospect of course, that it was 'sufficient notice of the plague to come', referring to the atrocious weather later that year in central European countries, which saw the Elbe in flood, many buildings undermined and a massive loss of life.[25]

A 'great comet with a tail' came in 1501 from the north to the district of Waldsassen monastery (G), and was seen for several days. Its chronicler recorded that it was 'A horrible sight which affected the minds of many, thinking that it foretold wars and death to come'. That did not happen, but it was followed by another comet around the feast of the Assumption (15 August), 'passing to the east, and having a tail with five barbs'. The chronicler wrote: 'It was a por-

---

[23] CF, p. 506; ACC, p. 282, respectively. These two chronicles, though differently named, are in fact one and the same.
[24] RCC, p. 88.
[25] CZ, pp. 230–2 (CXXVI, CXXVIII).

Eclipses

tent undoubtedly of the wars which ensued the next year'.[26] It is clear that the coming of comets, perhaps some years apart and unexpected, must have been injurious to the mental health of many.

ECLIPSES

There are many notices in the chronicles of eclipses, partial or total, of both the sun and the moon. A partial eclipse was described in 1132 by the chronicler of Fossanova (I) as 'the sun being seen as having a circle like an arc'.[27] A total eclipse might last a long time: the chronicle of Coggeshall (E) notes the consequent darkness as lasting for six hours in 1133, and for eight hours in 1190.[28] The chronicler of Kołbacz (P) left no doubt as to the day and time a comet appeared in 1321: it was 'on the day of John and Paul, at the third hour, *feria sexta*', in other words at about 9 am, on Friday, 26 June that year.

Eclipses must have been for many, not perhaps understanding what was happening, a time of alarm, especially when, as for 12 February 1161, the chronicler of Louth Park (E) recorded 'a terrible and protracted eclipse of the sun'.[29] The chronicler of Margam (W) told how, on 20 March 1140, at the ninth hour, an eclipse occurred 'while people were sitting at the

[26] *CW*, p. 82.
[27] *ACC*, p. 283.
[28] *RCC*, pp. 9, 30, respectively.
[29] *CLP*, p. 7.

table, and mentally very numb': in other words, they were slow to realise what was happening![30]

The Fossanova chronicler noted eclipses of the moon in 1103 ('in a cloudless sky'), and both versions of his chronicle told of the moon being obscured 'for three hours at the beginning of the night' on Candlemas Day (2 February 1143), and at other times.[31] There was an occasion, in 1117, when 'the moon appeared blood-red in the night'.[32]

HEAT AND DROUGHT

The well-being of medieval men and women in the matter of obtaining food supplies was very dependent on the weather; extremes either way could lead to widespread famine. The chronicles refer more often to an excess of rain than to a shortage of water. There were notable exceptions: the chronicle of Louth Park (E) mentions that in 1114 'the River Thames was dried up';[33] that of Fossanova (I) related that 1168 had 'a summer of drought';[34] the chronicle of Waldsassen records that in 1251, from around the feast of Ss Peter and Paul (29 June), and for about fifteen days, 'there was intolerable heat, day and night, and

---

[30] *AM*, p. 14.
[31] *ACC*, pp. 281, 283, 286–7; *CF*, p. 509.
[32] *CLP*, p. 4.
[33] *CLP*, p. 3.
[34] *CF*, p. 515.

Thunderstorms and Lightning

many religious and laity died';[35] and the chronicle of Zbraslav (C) informs us that in 1307 'drought in Bohemia led to a downturn in agricultural produce, and many died'.[36]

THUNDERSTORMS AND LIGHTNING

Bad weather was the cause of the dedication of the abbey church of Stams (A) having to be postponed from the 3 November to the 21st in 1284.[37] The chronicler of Coggeshall (E) told of several violent storms. One, a thunderstorm in 1176, 'caused hens to lay an abundance of hard eggs'! Another came on the morrow of St John the Baptist (25 June) in 1201, when 'terrific storms with thunder and lightning, lasting for fifteen days, felled men, animals and crops, burnt houses and threw down trees', to be followed by severe flooding 'with bridges broken, and crops submerged'. Four years later, 'on the night of St John the Baptist', and especially in the Maidstone area of Kent, were 'horrendous thunder and terrific lightning', whilst 'an intolerable smell came from the bodies of dead animals'.[38]

The annals of Margam (W) recounted a great storm in 1222, 'in the night after the feast of St Lucy' (13

---

[35] *CW*, p. 344.
[36] *CZ*, p. 36.
[37] *CKS*, p. 32.
[38] *RCC*, pp. 18, 129, 155, respectively.

December), when even oak tees were felled.[39] In 1228 or thereabouts, the bishop of London was officiating in St Paul's Cathedral, when there came 'thunder and lightning, and an intolerable stench'. The congregation went out, and the bishop was left alone with his ministers.[40]

Lightning caused several monastic fires, but others resulted from neglect or accident or arson. In Wales, in 1223, 'perverse men burnt within one week more than a thousand of Margam's sheep'.[41] In Belgium, in 1571, the country people of Westcapelle and Ramscapelle, having adopted the Protestant reform, totally destroyed the abbey of Ter Doest by fire.[42] Saddest of all, when arson in 1472 did much damage to churches and other buildings in Erfurt, Martisburg and Naumburg, the principal culprit turned out to be none other than a monk of nearby Pforta abbey.[43]

The chronicler of Coggeshall (E) told how on Christmas night in 1172 there was 'a horrible noisy thunderstorm and lightning throughout England and Wales'.[44] The annals of Waverley (E) ceased in 1291, so it was the chronicler of Louth Park who related that in 1311 the abbey church of Waverley was 'consumed by fire from the stroke of a thun-

---

[39] *AM*, p. 33.
[40] *CMM* 1, p. 443.
[41] *AM*, p. 34.
[42] *CTD*, p. 28.
[43] *CP*, pp. 149–50.
[44] *RCC*, p. 16.

derbolt'.[45] A 'terrible storm and lightning damaged the abbey church walls' at Waldsassen (G) in 1504.[46]

The chronicle of Strata Florida abbey (Ystrad-fflur) in Wales ceased at the year of 1281, at the height of the Edwardian Conquest of Wales, so we must turn to that of the Benedictine abbey of St Werburgh, Chester, to find what happened at Strata Florida in 1284: 'Within ten days of Christmas, lightning struck the belfry, burning the whole of it, and then the whole church, except the presbytery, miraculously preserved as the body of Our Lord was kept there on the great altar, under lock, as elsewhere is the case, according to universal custom'.[47] There were, of course, no fire engines in those days!

GALES

Especially in an age when some buildings may not have been as strongly built as is now the case, violently strong winds could do much damage. A few examples from the chronicles must suffice. The first is from the annals of Margam (W), which relate that on 17 October 1089, a furious wind in London destroyed more than six hundred houses, and lifted off the roof of the church of St Mary-at-Bow, burying two men there.[48]

---

[45] *CLP*, p. 24.
[46] *CW*, p. 79.
[47] *SWW*, pp. i–ii, 153, 197.
[48] *AM*, pp. 4–5.

The annals of Henryków (P) report a violent blizzard in 1318, which descended about the hour of Vespers 'on the 11th of the kalends of January [22 December], making it impossible for men on the road or in the fields to reach home. Many perished'.[49] The same chronicle tells us that in 1386, on the 'day of Agnes secunda [28 January] a great wind from the north, not known for a hundred years, hurled the great church bell to the ground'.[50] At Croxden (E) on 1 February 1373, a 'tempestuous strong wind removed the lead from the dorter, infirmary and abbot's chamber', as well as felling half the trees in the orchard, thirty oaks at 'Gret', and its tithe-barn at Spon.[51]

FLOODING

Most Cistercian monasteries had a riverine location, some a lacustrine, and a few a marine setting, which gave them a water-supply, the possibility of drainage channels and of mill leats, and fishing and transport by their own boats, but such a low-lying site rendered them at potential risk from flooding. It was a possibility foreseen in the mid-twelfth century by the third abbot of Pforta (G), Adelold, in his negotiations with a local landowner.[52]

---

[49] *AH*, p. 546; *RCH*, p. 703.
[50] *RCH*, p. 704.
[51] *ACK*, p. 308.
[52] *CP*, p. 49.

Flooding

On 11 July 1233, 'at the sixth hour', came a 'terrible tempest' throughout England. The water of the River Wey in Surrey rose by eight feet, and ran through the monastery of Waverley, which lay on its bank.[53] In 1323 an unexpected deluge of rain flooded Altenberg monastery (G), 'even entering the church, and destroying the books in the choir and the library'.[54] At Walkenried (G) in 1409, 'storm clouds' led to the inundation of the monastery: 'all present were in danger of death, and the animals in the stables suffocated'.[55] When, in 1337, the adjacent River Inn 'flooded greatly', Stams (A) was more fortunate, as a new channel cut by the abbey, and 'the efforts of the abbot and his monks', averted immediate danger'.[56] Meaux abbey (E) constructed a flood-gate at 'Hullam', to stop excess water from the river Hull drowning the marshes, peat bogs and pastures, at its villages of Waghan and Sutton.[57]

The chroniclers also recorded major floods from rising river levels throughout Europe, with the consequences for the local populace. The annals of Fossanova (I) record that when in 1180 the River Tiber overflowed, many houses were submerged, and 'innumerable serpents were drawn out'.[58] Flooding by the River Rhine finds repeated mention in the

[53] *CW*, p. 312.
[54] *CMC*, p. 306.
[55] *CWK*, p. 157.
[56] *CKS*. 128.
[57] *CMM* 1, p. 411.
[58] *ACC*, p. 287; *CF*, p. 515.

Cistercian Chronicles and Necrologies

chronicle of Camp (G), as in 1279, 1312, 1496 and 1497.[59] Remarkably, it tells how in perhaps 1279, the river flooded so badly, that 'boats entered over the city walls of Cologne'. In Poland, in 1430 (on 1 April) the River Vistula burst its banks by Werder island, and flooded parts of Danzig (Gdańsk), as did the River Radun in 1500.[60]

In England, the extremely low-lying Fenland in East Anglia was especially liable, as in 1255, when, on the morrow of the feast of St Dionysius (10 October), severe flooding affected the localities called Holderness, Holland and Lindsey.[61] The Fenland was also open to danger from the North Sea, as when, in 1287, 'the church of St Peter, Mablethorpe, was rent asunder by the waves of the sea'.[62] In 1177 the sea invaded the country of Holland, and 'submerged innumerable men, villages and pastures', as noted in the chronicle of Waldsassen (G).[63] The chronicle of Aduard (H) tells of the sea flooding part of Frisia in 1218,[64] and the annals of Oliwa (P) note that a great storm in 1500 destroyed thirty ships, presumably in the Baltic.[65]

---

[59] *CMC*, pp. 295, 300, 348–9.
[60] *AO*, pp. 376, 375, respectively.
[61] *CLP*, p. 16; *CMM* 3, pp. 120–1 (in Holderness in the 1360s, the sea removed the church and hamlet of Ravensere).
[62] *CLP*, p. 19.
[63] *CW*, p. 241.
[64] *CA*, p. 54.
[65] *AO*, p. 375.

Summer Rains

SUMMER RAINS

A good summer helped to ensure the well-being of a people. The annalist of Waverley told that in 1288 there was 'an abundant harvest in all England',[66] whilst the chronicler of Louth Park said of 1339 that there was 'such an abundance of produce'.[67] He adds, however, that in 1149, 1151, 1158 and 1258, the harvest of crops in England 'was destroyed by excessive rain'.[68] The annals of Croxden (E) are more explicit: in 1330, 'before and after an eclipse of the sun came such heavy rain for months that in many places the harvest did not mature until Michaelmas [29 September]', whereas in 1332 good conditions allowed the harvest 'to be gathered in by St Bernard's Day [20 August], and sowing to be ended by St Dionysus [9 October]'.[69]

FROST AND ICE

There are a number of references in the chronicles to extremely severe winters in northern Europe from time to time, yet another factor decreasing agricultural output. Blizzards could be more than a nuisance. The chronicler of Waldsassen (G) related how

[66] *AW*, p. 408.
[67] *CLP*, p. 36.
[68] *CLP*, pp. 5, 6, 17.
[69] *ACK*, p. 305.

from 14 December 1241 ('the morrow of St Lucy'), heavy snow, developing into a blizzard, fell until Christmas Eve, and 'exhausted man and beasts'.[70] The annals of Oliwa (P) relate that as late in 1443 as the feast of Ss Philip and James (1 May), a great deal of snow fell on Danzig (Gdańsk) 'and shocked and frightened many'.[71]

The Coggeshall chronicle tells us that, from 10 December 1151 to 19 March 1152, a great frost caused the River Thames in London to freeze over, and men and horses could cross upon the ice. The same happened from 1 January until 25 March in 1205 (and indeed in the 1740s).[72] The annals of Fossanova (I) tell how over the winter of 1167–8, Lake Fucine in Abruzzo, seventeen by eleven kilometres in size, froze, and again 'men could pass across it'.[73] The chronicle of Zbraslav (C) refers to the freezing of local rivers, and people walking across them on the ice, from the feast of St Andrew (30 November) in 1316 until Palm Sunday (28 March) in 1317, but also told of 'the great hunger, both of man and beasts'.[74]

The seas could also be affected. The annals of Kołbacz abbey (P) told of a severe winter in 1323, when many died, but one 'could cross on the ice from Slavia to Dacia', possibly a reference to the north-

---

[70] *CW*, p. 329.
[71] *AO*, p. 365.
[72] *RCC*, pp. 13, 151.
[73] *ACC*, p. 286; *CF*, p. 514 (the lake was drained in 1878, and given over to agriculture).
[74] *CZ*, p. 233 (CXXVIII).

west coastline of the Black Sea?[75] The annals of Oliwa (P) tell that after the feast of the Purification (2 February) in 1455, 'a severe frost even congealed the sea as far as Hel'. Hel is the settlement at the extreme end of the Hel peninsula, and some twenty miles from the mainland. Alas, the ice in the River Vistula having melted, its waters flooded 'the gardens of Gdańsk' the following Holy Week.[76] The chronicler of Camp (G) relates that in 1496 'the sea [perhaps referring to the Baltic] was frozen to a depth of twelve feet, ships were unable to sail, and were damaged by the ice';[77] water of course expands when it freezes.

PESTS, PLAGUE AND PESTILENCE

Plants, animals and humans suffered from time to time from devastating pestilences of one kind or another. Where animals were concerned their disease was generally referred to as 'murrain', described by the *Oxford English Dictionary* as being 'redwater fever or a similar infectious disease'. Whatever its nature, it was highly contagious, and there were no veterinary surgeons in those times to advise and assist! The chronicle of Louth Park (E) recorded, of 1156, 'a grievous murrain among animals and cattle'.[78] Information deriving probably from Tintern

---

[75] *AC*, p. 717: ancient Dacia was the lower Danube basin.
[76] *AO*, p. 363.
[77] *CMC*, p. 348.
[78] *CLP*, p. 6.

(W) told how, in 1319, 'a severe murrain killed cattle and sheep, some men had none left'.[79]

As for crops in the field, the locust might be the cause of calamity. The chronicle of Stams (A) records that in 1338, and 'for fourteen continuous days, a vast multitude of locusts invaded the province' (of Austria).[80] The annals of Zwettl (A) tell of the same occurrence: 'At the time of harvest, a vast multitude of locusts came from the coastlands in a great mass; so densely did they fly that the earth was darkened, and the splendour of the sun was not able to penetrate, and all corn, wheat, rye, oats, and all pasture land, were devoured, and they brought maximum damage to the land'.[81] The chronicle of Stams tells of a further locust invasion in 1348, which devastated 'not only the Tyrol, but all Germany', and which was followed by 'a terrible earthquake'.[82]

'Plague' and 'pestilence' were practically synonymous terms when used in the chronicles, and there was an understanding that disease could be infectious, and carried in the air. The chronicle written at Coggeshall (E), tells of a plague in 1192 in the Holy Land, 'after the victory of King Richard and when he stayed at Jaffa'. It was 'a certain morbid and contagious plague which came from corruption in the air'.[83]

---

[79] FHT, p. 343.
[80] CKS, p. 130.
[81] AZ, p. 683: the calendar of Zwettl (p. 691): 'around the time of the Assumption'.
[82] CKS, p. 138.
[83] RCC, p. 51.

THE BLACK DEATH

The chronicler of Oliwa (P) agreed. Writing of the Black Death, he suggested that the plague was especially prevalent where the transmission of infection might be marked, 'as in cities and maritime areas'.[84] Many people in the towns were perhaps poor and living in cramped conditions; the coastlands might see ships carrying the disease from one port to another. This chronicler also related that astrologers blamed the Black Death on the evil appearance of the planets Mars and Saturn.

This devastating and well-remembered disease, caused by a bacillus called *Yersinis pestis*, was rampant by the mid-1340s in parts of Asia, especially in India and China, and reached Italy by sea in 1348. It was very perceptive of the chronicler of Oliwa (P) to have known this, and to be able to give a lengthy account of its origins and transmission. He recounted that it came 'from the province of India, and spread to Greece, then on to Cilicia and Italy, being especially severe in Tuscany, and greatly affecting Prussia and Pomerania in 1349'.

The chronicle of Kaisheim (G) suggests an earlier coming of the plague, namely in 1347, telling of 'great pestilence everywhere', including the Netherlands, Hungary, and 'Welschland' (the Romansch-speaking parts of Switzerland). The plague did not depart

---

[84] *CO*, pp. 345–8.

quickly. It devastated the monastery of Kaisheim itself, from 18 March to the 7 April 1350, and of its community, fourteen monks, two novices, and six *conversi* died.[85] The chronicler of Meaux (E) recorded that the abbot, twenty-two of its monks and six *conversi* died in August 1349; only ten monks were left.[86] It also tells of the plague being in Ireland and Wales by 1349, and also at the port of Bristol, a probable entry point.[87]

The chronicler of Oliwa (P) noted three stages in the disease: 'First, it affected the lungs; then the arms, and then internal organs'. It was highly infectious, and so he continues: 'Medics did not visit the sick, neither did a father his son, nor a mother her daughter'.[88] The annalist of Aiguebelle (F) wrote that 'The malady paralysed the body, and was accompanied by malign fevers, and that in some villages remained alive only a tenth or a twentieth of the inhabitants'. Properties of Aiguebelle abbey at Pierlatte, Montélimar, Saint-Paul and elsewhere were transformed into hospitals to care for the sick.[89]

OTHER PLAGUES

There was a recurrence of the Black Death in 1361, which certainly reached as far west as the border

---

[85] CK, pp. 130, 132; his dating may be erroneous.
[86] CMM 3, pp. 37, 69.
[87] CMM 3, pp. 58–9.
[88] CO, pp. 345–8.
[89] AA, pp. 236–7.

Other Plagues

between England and Wales. The chronicler of Louth Park (E) related that 'It was a mortality chiefly affecting young men and boys, commonly called "the boys' pestilence"'. An earlier severe plague from 1312 to 1315 relayed by the chronicler of Schöntal (G) saw many people in Germany die, including 30,000 in Cologne, 14,000 in Basle, and 13,000 in Strasbourg. This was caused by plague, and the associated problems of 'hunger and starvation'.[90]

Five further 'pestilences' must be briefly mentioned. The chronicle of Aduard (H) tells that Mennard, its nineteenth abbot, died from a plague in 1421, whilst in Groningen.[91] 'Around the feast of Pentecost' in 1429 [15 May] there was a 'great plague' in the monastery at Camp (G); in a short time two priors, twelve other monks, a novice, two *conversi*, and some of the familiars had all died.[92] Of 1439, the chronicler of Riddagshausen (G) reported that 'a dreadful pestilence' had killed thirty-six of its monks.[93] The annalist of Oliwa (P) told that a severe disease in Danzig (Gdańsk) in 1464, had meant the burial of 5,800 people by the feast of Ss Simon and Jude [28 October].[94] Monks of Aiguebelle (F) died, when from 1530 to 1533 the 'sweating sickness' ravaged its neighbourhood.[95]

---

[90] CS, pp. 66–7.
[91] CA, p. 63.
[92] CMC, p. 318.
[93] CR, p. 53 (might this date be mistaken for 1349?).
[94] AO, p. 367.
[95] AA, pp. 319–20.

FAMINE AND A RISE IN FOOD PRICES

When agricultural output was diminished, food prices went up, and many people, especially the poor, suffered greatly from hunger, and died prematurely. The chronicler of Tintern (W) mentioned of 1316 that heavy summer rain that year meant a poor harvest, and 'a death rate of the poor not seen for a century'.[96] On 30 December 1202, a severe tempest in Italy destroyed property and woodland. There was later 'a lack of corn, and through much of Italy famine resulted'.[97] The chronicler of Waverley (E) told that in 1203 a major famine saw many die, and its monks dispersed to other houses.[98] For 1225, the chronicles of Coggeshall and Louth Park recorded 'a great famine'.[99]

The chronicler of Zwettl (A) related that from 1281 to 1282 a dreadful plague and famine prevailed throughout Bohemia and spread to Austria: 'Monks of suffering houses had to be dispersed to other houses; without agriculture the fields lay barren, the stench of death filled the air; brother had to dig grave for brother, but the cemeteries could not take all the dead; rodents fed on the carcasses of dead horses and other animals'.[100]

---

[96] FHT, p. 340.
[97] ACC, p. 296; CF, p. 529.
[98] CW, p. 255.
[99] RCC, p. 8; CLP, p. 4.
[100] CZ, pp. 17–18 (XII).

Famine and a Rise in Food Prices

As recorded in the chronicle of Camp (G), plague and famine was the lot of Germany in 1317 and 1318, where 'many villages and houses had no inhabitants remaining'.[101] Nor were Poland and Silesia immune. The annals of Henryków (P) tell that innumerable Poles perished, that the cemeteries of Wrocław were full, and that many had to be buried outside the city.[102]

The quantity of available food was reflected in varying prices. Information from Louth Park (E) and Tintern abbeys (W) tell us that in years of abundant harvest (as 1339) one quarter of corn cost two shillings, but in years of severe famine (1316–17) one quart of wheat had been priced at 16 shillings, a quart of barley at 12 shillings, and of oats at five shillings.[103] The chronicle of Coggeshall records that in 1205, 'money had decreased in value'.[104]

During the plague of 1312–15 in Germany, 'a measure of corn increased in price to five silver marks', but the chronicler of Stams does not tell us the previous costing.[105] Of the tempest, lack of corn, and subsequent famine from 1202 to 1203 in Italy, the annalist of Fossanova informs us that a 'measure' of grain was sold for sixteen Provins pounds.[106] When in the 1340s 'a horrible famine' reigned in the region of Aiguebelle (F), 'a setier of wheat cost two florins,

---

[101] *CMC*, p. 304.
[102] *AH*, p. 540.
[103] *CLP*, p. 36; *FHT*, p. 530.
[104] *RCC*, p. 15.
[105] *CS*, pp. 66–7.
[106] *ACC*, p. 296.

and the florin was valued at forty-five sols':[107] but from what level?

EARTHQUAKES

These earth movements, little understood at the time, affected the monasteries as much as they did the outside world. The Coggeshall chronicler (E), writing of the year 1132, told of an earthquake in which 'the land was seen to subside, and horrific noises were heard coming from beneath the land'.[108] The annalist of Zwettl (A) recorded of 1348 'a great earthquake, in Carinthia, Styria and Carniola, up to the sea, such as is not remembered in our lifetime'.[109]

Cistercian chronicles recorded numerous other earthquakes, as in Italy in 1117, 'throughout Lombardy, with many buildings collapsing', and in 1170, 'A powerful earthquake which destroyed the walls of cities, and caused church bells to ring'.[110] An earthquake in East Anglia (E) around 1180 was also felt in Norway.[111] Some people asleep in England, perhaps in the year 1382, had a rude awakening, for an earthquake occurred 'at the hour of slumber'.[112]

---

[107] *AA*, p. 236: a *setier* in the Paris region equalled 12 bushels/140 pounds.
[108] *RCC*, p. 9.
[109] *AZ*, p. 684: i.e. basically south-east Austria.
[110] *ACC*, pp. 282, 286; *CF*, p. 507; *RCC*, p.7.
[111] *CMM* 1, p. 181.
[112] *CLP*, p. 26.

Earthquakes

In 1329, of a great earthquake in Bavaria and Bohemia, Abbot Peter of Zwettl (A) wrote: 'In our house in Prague, about the hour of Compline, the stone walls were broken down, and myself and those with me were filled with the greatest horror'.[113] The abbot included in the chronicle a lengthy letter from an astronomer linking such events with others of the previous autumn when there had appeared 'a comet of horrible appearance', followed by eclipses of both sun and moon. Alas, while the events he describes are attributed to 1329, his letter bears (perhaps as a mistake) the date of 1322.

Of 1301, 'on the day of Mary Magdalene' (22 July), the chronicler of Croxden (E) recorded 'a strong earthquake about the sixth hour, when all the brethren were at the first refection (mixt/breakfast), which unexpectedly brought unhoped for terror'.[114] On Passion Sunday, 1349 (29 March that year, and in the midst of the Black Death), the chronicler of Meaux (E) told how whilst 'Vespers was being chanted an earthquake projected the monks out of their stalls to lie prostrate on the ground'.[115] In 1443 an earthquake struck at Mogiła (P) one day during the chanting of Sext; 'the monks standing in their stalls, they fled from the church for fear and fright'.[116]

---

[113] *CZ*, p. 295 (XXII).
[114] *ACK*.
[115] *CMM* 3, pp. 37, 69.
[116] *CTM*, p. 461.

CONCLUSION

On the Black Death, the chronicler of Louth Park (E) recorded of 1349 that 'The hand of the only Omnipotent God struck the human race with a certain deadly blow',[117] and the disastrous 'heavy rain' of 1316, was seen by the chronicler of Zwettl (A) as coming 'at the disposition of God' (i.e. 'at His pleasure').[118] The people did not blame God; rather, at Avignon and elsewhere the chronicler of Oliwa (P) told how they held penitential processions to ward off the plague.[119] The annalist of Henryków (P) wrote that once the severe famine of 1317 had passed in Poland, the people of Wrocław erected a church there in honour of the Body of Christ.[120] It is known that, perhaps until around the year 1400, there were lengthy spells of warm weather which allowed viticulture in the far south of England, yet, as the foregoing shows, there were recurrent spells of cold climate throughout Europe.

---

[117] *CLP*, p. 348.
[118] *CZ*, pp. 230–2 (CCXVI, CXXVIII).
[119] *CO*, p. 348.
[120] *AH*, p. 540.

✥ PART B ✥

CISTERCIAN NECROLOGIES

What have they to tell us?

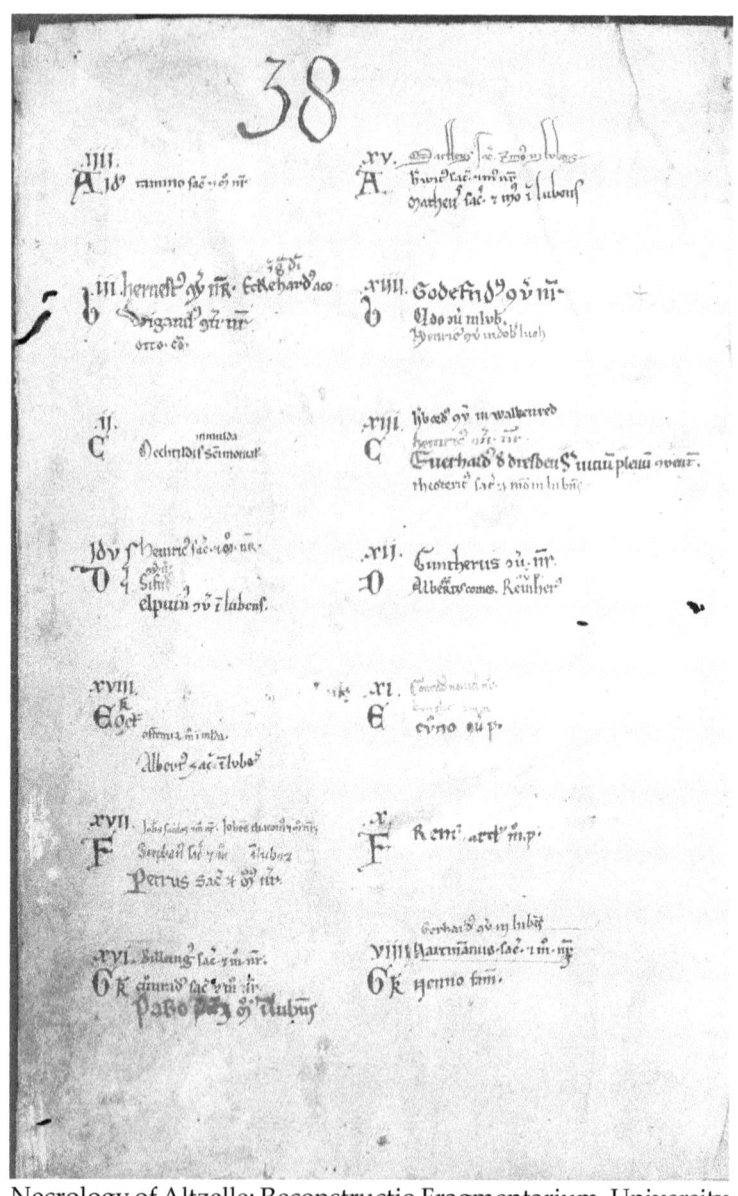

Necrology of Altzelle: Reconstructio Fragmentarium, University of Fribourg, Switzerland, lat 183, lat. 208, MS 38, ff. 1–2 (https://fragmentarium.ms/overview/F-7uj1). The manuscripts are held by Leipzig University Library. (This folio includes commemorations of Cistercians of other houses, including Matthew, 'priest and monk of Lubiąż', and Herbord, *conversus* of Walkenried').

INTRODUCTION

The early constitutions of the Cistercian Order laid down that at the daily chapter meeting a 'Commemoration of All Deceased Brothers and Familiars of our Order' be made, concluding with the words, 'May they rest in peace', the hearers responding 'Amen'. The preamble to the necrology of Sorø (D) also tells how 'on Sundays at Chapter, after the reading of a chapter of the Rule, the cantor reads the names of the deceased, as in the book, always commencing at the Sunday letter'; then followed a psalm and prayer for the dead. Another source has the necrology being read 'each week or every day after Prime'.[1]

This essay restricts itself to the evidence from necrologia, but for certain monasteries much more information can be gained from the encyclopaedic biographies of individual abbots, as for example the earlier version of the *Series Abbatum Ebracensium* for the abbots of Ebrach (G),[2] *Series D. D. Abbatum Runensium* for the abbots of Rein (A),[3] and the list (but only of successive names) given in *Moravia Sacra Historia* for Velehrad (C).[4] Another fulsome account

---

[1] Les *'Ecclesiastica Officia' cisterciens du XIIème siècle*, ed. D. Choisselet and P. Vernet, La Documentation Cistercienne 22, Oelenburg Abbey, Reiningue, 1989, pp. 204–5; *NSR*, pp. 577–8; *NBM*, p. xv.
[2] *Brevia Notitia Monasterii Ebracensis*, Rome, 1739, pp. 98–196.
[3] *Diplomatari Sacra Ducatus Styriae* 2, ed. J. F. C. Christian, Vienna, 1756, pp. 45–54.
[4] Ed. J. G. Stredowsky, Salzburg, 1710, p. 23 (48 abbots named

is to be found for the abbots, officers and monks of Bebenhausen (G), which has a description of the abbatial seals, but gives individual dates of death only infrequently.[5]

Several necrologies display fewer deaths in summer than in the winter months; as at Ląd (P): thirty-nine monks deceased in January as opposed to twenty-nine in July; forty-seven *conversi* as contrasted to twenty-six, and at Żarnowiec (P), thirty-two nuns as compared to but twelve. For the month of January, eleven monastic deaths were recorded at Engelszell, but only six in July. For the nunnery of Baindt relatively few anniversaries are recorded between June and October, suggesting more nuns died in the winter months. At Soleilmont, noteworthy is the fact that only fifteen died in the months of May and June. The necrology of Sorø is incomplete, but half of the names of the deceased familiars given occur in the month of January alone.[6]

The necrologies of some abbeys are no longer extant, save in fragmentary form: those of L'Arrivour (F) and L'Aumône (F) are no more, but a list of the abbots of the former derived from it is known.[7] A list exists of all the known medieval nuns of Ichter-

[5] from 1204 to 1699).
J. Sydow, ed., 'Die zisterzienserabtei Bebenhausen', in *Germania Sacra*, N.F., 16, 1984, pp. 223–97.
[6] NLA, *passim*; NOL, *passim*; NE, *passim*; NBT, *passim*; NSO, passm; NSR, *passim*.
[7] NAV, p. 332.

Introduction

hausen (G), but many of the dates seem to refer to their actual presence, rather than to their deaths.[8]

The importance of true necrologies is that they often supplement the information given in a monastery's charters or chronicle. It is inevitable, given the circumstances of the times, that there may be errors and exaggerations in a few necrologies. The 'book of the dead' of Bronnbach (G) relates that in 1632, 'Andrew, Bishop of Bamberg, was killed by the Swedes in another place'.[9] The bishop of that time was John George Fuchs; perhaps he took the name of Andrew on his episcopal consecration? In fact, he fled to Austria when the Swedes and soldiers of Saxony overran Bamberg in 1632, and there he died from a stroke early in 1633.

Necrologies may be known by other names, such as obituary, *obit* book, martyrology, or, in German, *Totenbuch*. The contents vary greatly, from perhaps little more than a list of departed abbots or a calendar with minimal information, to a much fuller account of the deaths of all religious and of benefactors—citing their gifts and grants. A drawback for this study is that in many instances, whilst the month and day of death are recorded, the year is not. This makes it impossible to determine, in the later Middle Ages, the period when the importance of the *conversi vis-à-vis* that of hired servants declined. Frequently also, it

---

[8] W. Rein, ed., 'Kloster Ichterhausen', in *Thuringia Sacra* 1, Weimar, 1863.
[9] *NBR*, p. 94.

is not possible to arrange the deceased abbots named in chronological order.

SOURCES

The necrology of **Aldersbach** (G) derives from four manuscripts in the Library and the State Archives at Munich. The first, of the fourteenth century, lists the persons named in four columns: the abbots and other ecclesiastics, the monks, the *conversi*, and the familiars. The last section, perhaps of the sixteenth century, has additions up to the eighteenth.

The necrology of **Altenberg** (G) derives from the work of a monk of the house about 1760, and is based on two manuscripts from the abbey library: the first covers the period down to the fifteenth century, while the second has additions through to the eighteenth. The necrology contains frequent references to the Benedictines of Gottweig.

The necrology of **Altzelle** (G) survives only in three single folios and two double folios, covering the period from 1186 to 1250, and is now available online at Fragmentarium. Whilst most entries refer to religious, nobility is also included, such as the death of Queen Elizabeth of Hungary, assassinated in 1213. Practically all the entries are undated. The fragments were later used for paste-downs in some manuscripts of Altzelle.[10]

[10] Reconstructio Fragmentarium, University of Fribourg,

Sources

The obituaries of the nuns of **Argenton** (B) are conserved at the State Archives in Namur. The first dates from the sixteenth century, with the insertion of *obits* of the seventeenth. The second dates from the seventeenth century. The third, comprehending the first two, was redacted in 1759 and is utilised here.

A partial obituary has been published for **Aulps** (F), with entries mostly ranging from 1546 to 1721. It was firstly the compilation of Nicholas Grandat, subprior, and amended around 1718 by another monk, Claud Delagrange. It gives no details of benefactors, but it does note the dates of entry of its religious into the novitiate.

The *Totenbuch* of **Baindt** (G) has occasional reference to dates in the early Middle Ages, but mostly the entries date from the sixteenth and eighteenth centuries. The compilation ends with the words, 'Finis 1681', so it may be that the printed version is an expansion of an older compilation. The most recent entry tells of the death in 1836 of the last abbess, Maria Xavier.

The necrology of **Baudeloo** (B, Ghent University, MS 481, folios 2–46), which has the features of a calendar, reminds us of the number of days in each month, and highlights those which were feasts of twelve lessons, and in some cases of a sermon. It gives an almost complete list of superiors down to the 33rd abbot, who died in 1709. The Appendix

Switzerland, lat 183, lat. 208, MS 38, ff. 1–2. The original manuscripts are held by Leipzig University Library.

gives a complete listing of the monks of Baudeloo over the centuries.

A history of **Bebenhausen** (G) gives a fulsome account of the abbots of the monastery, with a description of their seals, and a list of the officers of the house, followed by a catalogue of its monks, but rarely gives their dates of death.[11]

The necrology of **Billigheim** (G) forms part of a much larger work, the *Book of Billigheim*, which reposes in the Landesbibliothek at Stuttgart. The script and internal evidence point to a date of compilation in the second half of the fourteenth century, earlier perhaps rather than later. This is especially suggested by the fact that the seventh and last abbess to be named died around 1350.

The necrology of **Boneffe** (B) bears the date of 1674, and was compiled by a monk of the house, J. Defex, then continued by other monks after his death until the forced closure of the abbey in 1794. Boneffe was a monastery where monks of the Order replaced their Cistercian sisters in 1470, and a complete list of its abbots is attached.

An early obituary of **Bornem** (B), prepared by the prior, Philip de Valcken, in 1668, is believed to have been lost when the church and cloister were burnt by fire in 1672. Another monk, Gerard Hoffman, renewed the work, and after his death in 1776 various monastic scribes carried on the task.

---

[11] 'Die Zisterzienserabtei Bebenhausen', ed. J. Sydow, *Germania Sacra*, N.F., 16, 1984, pp. 223–97.

Sources

The obituary of **Boulancourt** (F), drawn up in 1779 as an annex to its cartulary, tells mostly of significant clerics and laity, such as King Ildefonse of Castile and Count Thibaut of Champagne. An earlier Latin necrology is lost. That published includes the *obit* of Dame Antoinete of Vitry, 'who requested in her will of 1552, that her name be inscribed in the obituary'.[12]

The 'book of the dead' of **Bronnbach** (G) is partly based on a compilation in 1585 by John Aegitzerus, then prior, revised and corrected in 1699 by Fr Andrew Lang; the published version stretches to the profession of the last monk in 1801. The main necrology is followed by a list of anniversaries to be observed, and then by a catalogue of the 'fathers and brothers' of the period.

The lost necrology of **Cambron** (B) was in part at least the work of Marc Noël, once bursar of the monastery, and a monk there from 1596 until his death in 1653. The co-author was a priest and Cistercian chaplain, John of Assignien, who died in 1633. This listing contains the names of 646 abbots and monks and of 112 *conversi*, but their dates are mostly not stated. In the printed version, it is followed by a further list of religious taken from Fr Noël's notes, and then by a deed (never fully executed), commencing in 1651, naming seventy-three monks and twenty-four *conversi*.[13]

---

[12] *NBL*, p. 329.
[13] *NC*, pp. 100–32.

The original necrology of **La Cour-Dieu** (F) is unknown, but the published version, together with a list of abbots in chronological order, derives from manuscripts in the Bibliothèque Nationale, the Bibliothèque de l'Arsenal and the Bibliothèque d'Orléans, assisted by notes made previously by a monk of the house, Dom Estienne.

The obituary of **Croxden** (E) is referred to in 1691 in Henry Wharton's *Anglia Sacra*, where it is noted that the death of Geoffrey, Prior of Canterbury, is omitted from 'the Obituary of Crokesden'.[14] The necrology, as published,[15] is derived from the chronicle of the house, and apart from giving a list of its abbots, refers mostly to the *obits* of the founding De Verdun family.[16]

The **Brevia Notitia Monasterii B.V.M. Ebracensis** (G), published in Rome in 1739, and which caused some disquiet,[17] alludes to the necrology of the house, but without citing its location. The *Brevia* does recount the several abbots in the fullest terms, as also the sepulchral monuments in the abbey church. The published version, printed in 1902 in *Cistercienser-Chronik*, yields much information, and lists deceased religious arranged in groups for each successive abbacy. The opening section gives also the *obits* of the early abbots of Aldersbach, Bildhausen,

---

[14] H. Wharton, *Anglia Sacra* 1, London, 1691, p. 797.
[15] *MA* V, London, 1846, pp. 661–2.
[16] British Library, MS Cotton Faustina B6.
[17] *NEBR*, p. 267.

Sources

Heilsbronn, Langheim and Wilhering, all daughter foundations of Ebrach.[18]

Two necrologies make up the published version of the necrology of **Engelszell** (A). The first dates from the early fifteenth century; it was composed by Nicholas, a monk of the house, and was followed by further work in the early eighteenth century. The first necrology is arranged in four columns, listing firstly princes, bishops and abbots; secondly priests, monks and but a few *conversi*; thirdly nobility, and lastly familiars, servants and those in fraternity. There is note of at least seven vineyards, and *famulus* rather than *familiaris*.

The necrology of **Feldbach** (Sw) was first drawn up in the fifteenth century by Nicholas Kaermerli, a monk of Salem and confessor at Feldbach. He died in 1473 and later hands continued his work. There are very many entries of nuns, their parents and siblings.

An account of the necrology of **Frauenroth** (G) tells of twenty-four abbesses between around 1250 and 1557, names twenty-eight of its nuns and twelve known chaplains from 1264 to 1511, and notes twenty-five male *conversi* between 1264 and 1396, but very rarely gives their dates of death.[19]

The necrology of **Frauenthal** (Sw) is fragmentary. Its compilation was the work from 1623 of Brother Thomas Schöppelin, together with other seven-

---

[18] *NEBR*, pp. 130, 134, 200.
[19] 'Das Cistercienserinnen-Kloster Frauenroth', *Cistercienser-Chronik* 16, no. 182, 1904.

teenth-century scribes. Few dates are noted, but those which are range between 1234 and 1477. For the 'abbey', the term *Gotshus* ('God's house') is used.

The necrology of **Fürstenfeld** (G) lists the abbots of the house from Volkmar, the fifth abbot (who died in 1314, after an abbacy of thirty years), down to Leonard, the eighteenth abbot (who passed away in 1496). It omits any mention of the fifteenth abbot (possibly Abbot Herman), and also does not yield the dates of death of the thirteenth and fourteenth abbots (Andrew and Paul). The average length of an abbacy was seventeen years, and no recorded abbot served for fewer than ten years. The major part of the necrology, the manuscript now in the royal libray at Munich, was the work of John Zolner, monk of the house, in the mid-seventeenth century, and makes reference to 'the old martyrology'.

The original necrology of **Fürstenzell** (G), a manuscript in the royal library of Munich, speaks for itself: 'This present book of the familiars and benefactors of the monastery was revised in the year of Our Lord 1463, in the time of Abbot John, and of brothers Thomas Kunner, John Ferg and Hawg, who made this work until now'.[20] The published version has additional material through to the seventeenth century.

The necrology of **Hauterive** (Sw) exists in photocopy form, and I am grateful to Frère Michel of the monastery for supplying me with relevant pages.

---

[20] *NF*, p. 106.

Sources

Like other continental obituaries it has much to tell of the closure of the original community in 1848.

The compilation of the obituary of **Heiligenkreuz** (A) derives from three sources: firstly, an ancient necrology, covering the years down to 1260; secondly, a further composition instituted by Prior Matthias, stretching from 1260 to 1626, and the work of one George Lan; and, lastly, the list of pittances and anniversaries, put together in 1688 by George Strohl, a monk 'of optimum merit'. The published necrology is the work of the late Florian Watzel, when archivist of the monastery.

A published necrology for **Heilsbronn** (G) is restricted to the months from May to August for the thirteenth and fourteenth centuries. It tells nothing of the community, but of the laity and its pittances.

All that is left of the martyrology of **Herkenrode** (B) are five fragments on parchment and of Gothic script from the later thirteenth century, later used to bind other books. The emphasis is on the early martyrs of the Church, as in the entry for Ss Cosmas and Damian, for 27 September, telling how 'after many torments, they were bound and chained, and drowned in the sea'. It relates that Herkenrode was founded in 1192, and dedicated to St Michael the Archangel.[21]

The considerable fragment of the necrology of **Hohenfurt** (Vyšší Brod, C), more properly known as 'Die Rosenbergische Chronik des Jakob von

---

[21] *NHK*, f. 723r–723v.

Gratzen', was the work of a monk of the house, Jacob von Gratzen, and completed on St Lucy's Day (13 December) 1472. It deals primarily with the lives and bequests of members of the founding Rosenberg family.

The unpublished necrologies of Paszto, Pilis, Szent Gotthárd and Zirc, furnished me by Brother Nivard Halász of Zirc, reflect the expansion of the Ottoman Empire into much of **Hungary** in the early-sixteenth century, their monks taking refuge at Heiligenkreuz.

The necrology of **Jardinet** (B) is based in part on marginal notes of the thirteenth century in Bibliothèque Nationale, MS 5553, and compiled by M. Lex, archivist of Saône-et-Loire.[22]

The 'book of the dead' of **Jędrzejów** (*Andreovia*, P) appears to be compiled from a fourteenth-century 'book of the fraternity and confraternity', a compilation of 1629, and additions made perhaps at the close of the eighteenth century. The published version is preceded by a listing of the known abbots, and of the commendatory abbots who held the house between 1600 and 1735.

The necrology of **Kaisheim** (*Caesarea*, G) derives from the compilation of a monk of the house, Sebastian Zeller, up to his death in 1588, and its continuation by Mathias Hering, also a monk of the abbey.

---

[22] See also *Martyrologie et Chartes de l'Abbaye de Notre Dame du Jardin lez Pleurs*, ed. L. Lex, Troyes, 1885, pp. 5–8, where only a selection of entries from the original manuscript appears.

Sources

In its published form it owes much to Gabelkover, once royal archivist of Stuttgart.

The 'book of the dead' of the monastery of **Kamieniec** (*Kamenz*, P) is online in microfilm. The range of entries is from 1200 to 1769, but mostly they emanate from the seventeenth and eighteenth centuries, when it is clear that most of the religious were of German or Polish descent, though at least one monk came from Moravia. From the sixteenth century onwards the handwriting varies greatly. There is a great preponderance of the *obits* of family members of deceased religious and, interestingly, several monks in the later centuries had, or adopted on profession, the names of Caspar or Melchior, less often of Balthasar, such as Melchior Gelweten, prior for over forty years who died in 1682.[23]

The necrology of **Kołbacz** (P), as published, appears to have been extracted from the annals of the house.

The 'book of the dead' of **Koronowo** (P) is believed to have been made by Maciej Rajmund Garczyński in 1717, with further entries being added down to 1810. It included *obits* from both Byzsewa and Koronowo, to which the monks migrated in 1283, but its reliability has been questioned.[24] The published version encompasses a list of the abbots, the *obits* of monks

---

[23] *NKM*, image 54; *NB*, pp. 38v, 36v; *NPL*, pp. 65, 76, for the names of Caspar and Balthasar in the Baudeloo and Pelplin necrologies.

[24] Piotr Oliński, *Konwent Koronowski w Świetle Źródeł*, Toruń, 2003, p. 141.

from several other Polish Cistercian houses, a further biographical listing of the religious of Koronowo itself, an enumeration of those in confraternity with the monastery, and a brief listing of burials within the abbey church. The principal section tells of the deaths in the year 1774 alone of religious of the abbeys of Bledzew, Jedrzejów, Mogiła, Obra, Oliwa, Paradyż, Przemęt, Sulejów, Wąchock, and Wągrowiec, as well as the nunneries of Ołobok, Owińska and Vallis Angelica (the latter in what is now Belarus from 1743 to 1883).

The 'book of the dead' of **Ląd** (P) derives in large measure from the comprehensive necrology drawn up before his death in 1681 by Abbot Zapolski, commencing from 1545; in other words, once its German monks had left and migrated to Henryków. Additional notes were added up to the death of the prior, Tadaeus Wysocki, in 1842.[25]

The necrology of **Langheim** (G), as edited, is arranged in alphabetical order by Christian name, not in chronological order. It owes much to the work of Fr Georg Stroll, and to manuscripts in the monastery library.

The earliest manuscript for the necrology of **Lilienfeld** (A) was drawn up about 1270, and arranged in four parallel columns, listing respectively monks, nuns, *conversi*, familiars and others. A further compilation was made about 1639, by which time a number

---

[25] I am indebted to Dr A. Nienartowicz of Toruń for assistance with Polish translation.

of different hands had contributed to the manuscript. An additional recension was that by a monk of the house, Chrysostom Hanthaleg, in the early eighteenth century. There are two published versions, by Zeissberg in 1879 and by Fvchs in 1913. They differ very slightly. The one gives the *obit* of a benefactor, Heinrich Chastner, as being observed on 25 January, but the other ascribes his commemoration to the 3 February. The one notes the *obit* on 6 January of the organist, Robert Sindt, but not the other.

The work entitled *Epitome Fastorum Lucellensium* (F), published in Basle in 1667, notes the 'old and recent necrologies' of the monastery,[26] but without citing their whereabouts.

The necrology of **Marche-les-Dames** (B) covers only the later times of the convent; the entries are mostly of the seventeenth and eighteenth centuries. It is divided into two sections: the first part, recording clerical and professed religious, enumerates approximately 220 nuns, 120 *conversae*, four male *conversi*, 16 male familiars and 9 female familiars. The nunnery obviously enjoyed spiritual fraternity with the Crucifers (Crutched Friars) and canons of the Holy Cross at nearby Huy, and lists the *obits* of fifty-one of them. The second portion of the necrology refers to other religious of the house, and of the Crucifers naming another sixty-three, but its chief import is to name over five hundred relatives of the community granted an annual *obit*.

[26] NLC, f. 42, 44.

The obituary of **Maubuisson** (F) was redacted in 1671 with earlier manuscript evidence by D. Estiennot; his work now resides in the Bibliothèque de Pontoise. Whilst the successive abbesses are recounted, little is said regarding the lower ranks of nuns. The necrology gives prime place to monarchs and the nobility, such as King Philip (*ob.* 1285) and Queen Blanche (*ob.* 1252), its foundress, and also to ecclesiastical dignitaries.

The published excerpts from the 'book of the dead' of **Mogiła** (*Clara Tumba*, P) derive from a fifteenth-century compilation employed by a seventeenth-century copyist.

The fragmentary remains of the obituary of **Moulins** (B) are conserved in the State Archives at Namur. The abbey became a male monastery in 1414.

The necrology of **Neuberg** (A) covers the years from 1405 to 1846, lists 218 deceased religious in semi-chronological order, and is in part based upon a compilation made in 1750 by Fr Eugene Assem, who held the posts of prefect of the scholars, novice master and abbot's secretary.[27] After his death in 1765 Fr Ferdinand Hausenberger continued his work, which is preceded by the 'Names of Religious professed of this monastery who from 1603 died piously in the Lord'.

The necrology of **Neuencamp** (G), its *Totenbuch*, is but a fragment covering the months from 21 May to 15 July, and would seem to be no later than the fif-

---

[27] *NNB*, p. 44.

teenth century in composition. It gives a full detailed calendar for that part of the year.

The necrology of **Neuzelle** (G), kindly provided by Fr Konrad Ludwig, O.Cist., brings the record up to the present day, not only for that abbey, but also for other central European houses, including Heiligenkreuz, Lilienfeld and Vyšší Brod.

The register of **Newenham** (E), once in the Arundel Collection of the Royal Society, gives a brief necrology of its benefactors, followed by a detailed list of abbots.

The list of 'founders and principal persons', as published for **Newminster** (E), derives from the martyrology of that house, once forming part of the Cecil manuscripts.

The late-thirteenth-century necrology of the nunnery of **Notre-Dame-des-Prés by Douai** (F), now preserved in the Bénézech collection of the municipal library of Valenciennes, has been dated by one author to between 1293 and 1297, by another source to around 1325. Arranged in two columns, nuns *vis-à-vis* seculars, it lists sixty-six religious of noble, and one hundred and ninety-nine of patrician birth, reflecting its urban setting. The first section of a much larger work by Usuard, a monk of Saint-Germain du-Prés, the cost was borne by the Lenfant family of Douai.

The 'book of the dead' of **Oliwa** (P), giving the names of deceased religious and benefactors, as well as of the Cistercian sisters of Żarnowiec, was in large part compiled in 1615, with later additions made around 1793 and 1802–6. It says little about family members of the monks and nuns, but does reflect local political troubles.

The necrology of **Orval** (B) stretches from the death of the first abbot, Constantine, in 1145, down to the passing of the fortieth abbot, Laurence de la Roche, in 1637, and practically all the intervening superiors find mention. The register also tells of many benefactors and some individual monks, but fails to note any of the many *conversi* or familiars of the house. It appears to be of mid-seventeenth-century compilation, and taken from a small book loaned by a seminary.

The necrology of **Pairis** (F) is partly based upon its *Tabula Mortuorum* compiled in 1650 by Bernhard Buchinger, abbot of its mother-house of Lucelle, and a copy book of around 1730. Additions in 1537 were noted as being made 'in a Protestant hand'.

The original 'book of the dead' of **Pelplin** (P) was written and updated in the year 1402; further work followed in the seventeenth century. The published version is preceded by an account of the foundation of the abbey, and a listing of its abbots.

The earliest known necrology of **Port-Royal-des-Champs** (F), written in French, dates from around 1450, and with other sources enabled M. D. Estiennot to publish a fuller version in 1671. It gives details of all the abbesses but says little of their nuns. The main thrust of the necrology is the listing of numerous significant personalities, both clerical and lay. These are greatly expanded, on a monthly basis, in

Sources

the 500-page necrology published in Amsterdam in 1713, a century after the 'reform' of the abbey, and on embracing Jansenism. The voluminous supplement, published in 1735, gives copious notes of notabilities of the day as well as of the religious, and it tells of the early involvement of Sisters Marie-Magdalene (*ob.* 1684) and Sister Elizabeth de Ste Agnes (*ob.* 1706), 'in redacting the necrology, and putting in order the other papers of the abbey'.[28]

The original obituary of **Preuilly** (F) no longer exists, save for an eighteenth-century copy, which, owing to the diligence of French scholars of the time, enabled publication to take place. It says much of benefactors and notabilities, but little of the brethren of the house.

Nothing is written regarding the origins of the necrology of **Raitenhaslach** (G), but in part it would appear to have derived from the monastery's former Book of Oblations.

The necrology of the abbey of **Reclus** (F) survives as a solitary phrase relating to one of the abbots.

The necrology of **Rein** (A), based upon a manuscript of the close of the fourteenth century, is divided into five columns listing benefactors, monks, novices, *conversi* and familiars.[29] Twenty-one abbots of the house are named, only six bearing their date of death, whilst three are all named as having been the seventh abbot of the house. Supplementary information

---

[28] *NPRL* 2, p. 384.
[29] *NRE*, p. 341.

comes from the *Brevia Notitia* of its mother-house of Ebrach, relating that the first abbot of Rein, Gerlac, himself a monk of Ebrach, was 'a man of great virtue and of much wisdom'.[30]

The necrology of the nuns of **Roermond** (H) derives mainly from the researches of Charles Guillon, notary, and A. Farne.

The necrology of **St Servaas, Utrecht** (H), found in an 'old parchment book, with letters missing and damaged folios', and transcribed by Arnold van Buchel, lists between the death of the first abbess, Berta in 1284 and of Abbess Mechtild in 1482, the *obits* of twenty-two abbesses of the house, some one hundred nuns, almost twenty 'sisters' (*conversae*), and four male *conversi*. Additionally are listed very many relatives of the religious, such as John, brother of Katherine of Groenewoud, and Rotard, uncle of Margaret of Drakelin, both nuns.[31] Appended are two lists of those individuals enjoying spiritual fraternity with the community. There are no *obits* dated later than 1482, implying that this deed was written towards the close of the fifteenth century.

The martyrology of **St Stefano in Bosco** (I) is attributed to the thirteenth century. Cistercian from around 1150, the monastery became Carthusian from 1513.[32]

---

[30] *Brevia Notitia Monasterii Ebracensis*, Rome, 1739, p. 202.
[31] *NSS*, pp. 167, 169.
[32] A. Carolei, 'Il martirogio della Certosa di Santo SteL. M. Cerasoli', in *Archivio storico per la Calabria e la Lucania* XII, 1942; A. Carolei, 'Il martirologi della Certose di Santofano

Sources

The necrology of **St Urban** (Sw), the compilation of two monks, Leo and Pius, relates to the nineteenth century, and lists but thirty monks and a few lay-brothers.

The *Totenbuch* of **Salem** (A) owes much to two monks of the abbey, Matern Guldenmann, around 1450, and Eberhard Schneider, about 1769. It lists all forty abbots of the house, as well as over 800 monks and around 345 *conversi*. It also notes a few oblates, perhaps the equivalent of the medieval familiars, of whom nothing is written. It says little of benefactions to the monastery, but does give some insight into liturgical and other monastic information of its times. Each month is headed by the number of days it comprehends, as for January: 'January has 31 days, night hours 17, day 7'.[33]

There is no known necrology emanating from the abbey of **Sedlec** (C), but when in the later thirteenth century the Benedictine monastery of Podlážice in Bohemia was impoverished it pawned its very fine manuscript, the Codex Gigas, to Sedlec, but was able to redeem it in 1295. At the close of the volume is a calendar-cum-necrology, very probably of monastic origin, which makes much use of the Cistercian term for a lay-brother, *conversus*, and records the *obit* of one John, the abbot of Cistercian Osek, but any illusion that monks of Sedlec may have played a part in

---

[33] del Bosco', in *San Bruno di Colonia*, Rubettino, 2004, pp. 243–51. I am indebted for these references to Riccardo Cataldi, librarian of the monastery of Casamari.
NSL, p. 2.

compiling the necrology is dashed, for the 20 August makes no mention at all of St Bernard.[34] An outstanding extant manuscript is the necrology of **Seligenthal** nunnery (G). Originating perhaps in 1310, most of the entries relate to the later Middle Ages and to modern times. The listing of the dates for Easter Day suggests that some at least of the many post-dated entries were added in the seventeenth century: Easter came, the book reveals, in 1633 on 27 March. Apart from the lists of the deceased, the calendar notes the feasts of the apostles, and there is a section relating to benefactors and their gifts. In the fourteenth century, prominence is given to the *obits* of members of the princely family of Bavaria: as for Otto, 'the most serene king of Hungary and duke of Bavaria' (1313), and Otto, 'the illustrious duke of Bavaria' (1335). There is the occasional mention of a former abbess or nun, but also of laity who served the nunnery, such as in 1254 of Catherine Fraubergerin, 'our faithful waitress', and in 1259 the convent's doctor (John Raming) and apothecary (Philip Karthauser).[35] The version printed in *Necrologia Germaniae* IV has added lists of all known nuns, *conversae* and *conversi*.

---

[34] I am grateful to Johannes Fahlström, of the National Library of Sweden, Stockholm, where the volume is based, for sending me full internet cross references to a transcript of the codex.
[35] R. Kalcher, ed., *Die Urkunden des Klosters Seligenthal*, 1893, *passim*.

Sources

The nunnery of **Soleilmont** (B) possessed two necrologies: the one, kept in the church, was very incomplete; the other, kept in the chapter-house, was a full compilation by Alexander Morlet, a monk of Aulne in 1639. The published version has additions made to his work by later religious of the convent. One *obit* has the words, 'as is written in the old obituary in 1639'.[36] Most of the published entries are from the late sixteenth century through to the mid-nineteenth, listing 180 nuns. In the record are the names of 65 female *conversae*, 6 male *conversi*, 16 female familiars and 13 male familiars (one of them a priest).

The necrology of **Sorø** (D), compiled in 1518, exists as MS 868 in the Arnamagnæn Collection at the University of Copenhagen, and I am very grateful to Professor Matthew Driscoll for speedily sending me a copy of the printed version. It is not complete, as the folios covering the period between the 7th of the kalends of May (25 April) and the 16th of the kalends of July (16 June) are wanting. The preamble tells of the compilation as containing 'the names of the founders, familiars and benefactors of our monastery, as well as the names of the abbots, monks and *conversi*, who from the foundation until the present time have served the Lord in this place'. Only five abbots are noted, as well as a few nobles and benefactors; 27 familiars are listed, as well as 225 other persons, but very probably their names are mostly those of the *conversi*, though that is not specified.

---

[36] *NSO*, p. 391.

One scribe compiled the necrology of **Stams** (A) from the fifteenth century down to 1749; thereafter it was the work of another monk of the house, Anthony Kuprian.

The sixteenth-century necrology of **Tennenbach** (G) was lost in the various troubles of that abbey, and the published version derives from a copy fortunately kept in the archives of the monastery of Sankt Peter in Schwarzwald, Freiburg.

The necrology of **Tännikon** (*Lilienthal*, Sw), gives little information, apart from citing many names. Its compilation was due in part to a monk of Wettingen; the dates given range froom 1383 to 1482.

The fifteenth-century traveller and antiquary, William of Worcester, inspecting 'the ancient calendar of **Tintern**' (W), from an obituary listing the founder and his family, has little else to say, save that the building of the second and magnificent church owed much to the munificence of Roger Bigod, Earl of Norfolk and Lord of Chepstow.

The original of the obituary of **Val** (F) has been lost, but much of it was copied at the end of the seventeenth century, and this now reposes in the Bibliothèque Nationale in Paris. The entries date from around 1275; many *obits* are recorded, but little other information.

A number of *obits* relating to **Val-St-Lambert**, Belgium, appear in the margins of the folios of a thirteenth-century copy of the martyrology of Usuard, purchased in Brussels on 19 February 1857, and now forming Additional MS 18495 at the British Library,

Sources

London. Little detail is given of individuals, and a number of the entries are now scarcely readable, but included are the names of former abbots, local ecclesiastics, the parents of brethren, and citizens of Liège and Namur. A number of the *obits* are included within a stamped circular device.

The necrology of **Vauluisant** (F) is lost; only two extracts of seventeenth-century date survive.

The necrology of **Villers** (B) is of late date, covering only the period from 1574 to 1792, four years before the monastery was sacked and forced to close. It records the dates of death of 18 abbots and 363 monks, but not of *conversi*, familiars or benefactors. Much attention is paid to the later abbots of the period, their building works and the problems they faced. The necrology as published was communicated by M. Cuvelier, priest of Limal. Its authorship is to be credited to Bruno Cloquette, abbot from 1788, and his prior, Francis Blarian. Abbot Cloquette (*ob*. 1828) had been, successively, succentor, cantor, theologian and teacher of the juniors, and archivist.[37]

The necrology of the nuns of **Wald** (G) was written in the year 1505 by a nun of the house, Magdalene of Soffeln. Interestingly, this is another instance where gifts were noted as being made not to the monastery by title, but to 'God's house'.

The early years of the necrology of **Wettingen** (Sw) are in the twelfth-century hand of a monk, Herrgott, but the later compilation is in part the work of

---

[37] *NV*, pp. 86–7.

another monk, Rudolph of Hackberg, who died in 1423. Thereafter the necrology was completed by two different scribes in the seventeenth century. At the close there is an Index of Founders and Benefactors, listing no less than ninety-five donors.

The necrology of **Wilhering** (A), its *Totenbuch*, the work of several hands, with entries down to 1520, comes from two principal compilations, of 1345 and 1843. The published version is preceded by notes on the abbots of the house, whilst three lists of pittances follow the necrology.[38] A later source points to the compilations made by two monks of the house: John Long in 1462 and Willam Daz in 1654.

A calendar emanating from **Wintney** (E) gives the date of dedication of the nuns' church in 1243, and is the *obit* book of the convent. It lists just over one hundred nuns, including eleven former prioresses, some noted as being of 'good' or 'pious' memory, and ten *conversae*. It notes the deaths of six monarchs, six bishops of Winchester and six abbots of Reading, as well as the death of Abbot Adam of Waverley—who perhaps had oversight of the house.[39] It was compiled in 1729 by James West, based on the original material.[40]

The published necrology of **Zwettl** (A) derives from a twelfth-century obituary with additions made in the fourteenth and fifteenth centuries by various

---

[38] *NW*, pp. 177–204.
[39] The original manuscript is British Library, Cotton Claudius D.iii, f. 140v–162v.
[40] *NWN*, p. 393.

hands. The final major compilation was by Fr Bernard Hammerl, librarian and archivist of the monastery, 'a keeper of optimum merit'.[41]

FOUNDERS, MAJOR PATRONS AND BENEFACTORS

Most monastic necrologies tell of the founders of their houses, such as Wizlaus, prince of Rügen, who founded Neuencamp (G) in 1233; Duke Otto of Carinthia, who settled monks at Stams (A); and Baron Henry II of Rapperswil (*ob.* 1246), the effective founder of Wettingen (Sw). The *obit* of Margrave Leopold, founder of Heiligenkreuz (A), was to be observed each 15 November by 'Vigils seated, Terce from "Libera me", and Mass with all priests chanting'. The monks of Bornem (B) looked back to Duke Henry of Brabant (*ob.* 1233), the founder of St-Bernard-sur-l'Escaut (B), their first site, and interred at Villers, their mother-house.[42]

At Fürstenfeld (G), Duke Ludovic II of Bavaria (*ob.* 1294) was noted as being its 'first founder', and his wife Anne, who had died in 1271 and was buried in the choir, as its 'second founder'; obviously she had supported her husband in his enterprise. The necrology of Pairis (F) tells of Christian, abbot of Lützel (Lucelle, F), who died in 1138, shortly after

---

[41] *NZ*, p. 444.
[42] *NN*, p. 512; *NST*, p. 53; *NWT*, p. 590; *NH*, p. 111; *NWV*, p. 116; *RBM*, p. 101.

sending the first abbot and twelve monks to found Pairis. An *obit* list of Waverley (E), founded in 1128, shows that it supplied the first abbots of Ford (1136), Thame (1137), Bruern (1147) and Combe (1150), and presumably their requisite twelve monks.[43]

The founder of Rein (A), Margrave Leopold 'the Strong', died shortly after its initiation, and its necrology notes that his son, Ottakar, completed the foundation. The necrology of Lützel (Lucelle), tells of Bertulf of Neuchâtel, who died in 1129 and who had 'given freely' for the construction of the abbey, which, founded in 1124, was 'a fruitful olive planted in the house of the Lord'. The necrology of Wald (G) tells of Burchard of Wegkenstein as being its founder, and of his daughter, Judinta, as being the first abbess. The record of Seligenthal notes its first abbess, Agnes (1230–77), and an early prioress, Omelia Maria Maroltingerin (*ob.* 1254).[44] The necrology of Pilis (Hg) tells of Abbot John I (*ob.* 1256), who had acquired from King Bela IV a new confirmation of the monastery's privileges under a golden bull.[45]

The necrology of Pairis lists 'the illustrious Theobald, Duke of Brandenburg (*ob.* 1218), as an advocate of the monastery'. That of Jędrzejów (P) names several kings of Poland as being both 'benefactors and patrons', including Kings Władysław (*ob.* 1432), John Albert (*ob.* 1501) and Alexander (*ob.* 1506). That

[43] *NFN*, pp. 97, 100; *NPS*, p. 74.
[44] *NRE*, p. 352; *NLC*, pp. 29, 40; *NWD*, pp. 219, 221; *NS*, pp. 503, 509.
[45] *NHG*, non-paginated.

of Pelplin (P) informs us of Prince Casimir, king of Poland, who died in 1492: he was 'a singular benefactor, who had given to the value of one thousand marks to the monastery, and confirmed our privileges'.[46] That of Mogiła (P) tells of its foundation in 1222 by Bishop Iwo Odrowąż of Kraków, but also notes five other personages as having been 'founders', presumbly major benefactors at one time or another. The founders of Boulancourt, the count and countess of Béthel, were buried at the Cistercian abbey of Élan (F), but remembered at Boulancourt (F) with an *obit* Mass, and also on their anniversary by the recitation of fifty psalms.[47]

The family members of founders might be interred 'in the choir' or 'before the high altar'. This was especially true at Croxden abbey (E) and Vyšší Brod (Hohenfurth, C). The necrology of Croxden recorded the death of its founder, Bertram of Verdun, as occurring in 1192 on the feast of St Bartholomew (24 August). At least twelve members of the de Verdun family were buried at Croxden, amongst them Joan of Furnival, who died aged but thirty in 1334. She was interred before the high altar, 'between Nicholas de Verdun, son of the founder, and John of Verdun'. At Newenham (E), founders and benefactors who lay before the high altar, included Reginald de Mohun

---

[46] *NPS1*, p. 59; *NJD*, pp. 787–8, 792; *NPL*, p. 90.
[47] *NML*, p. 811, and *passim*; *NBL*, p. 531 (perhaps a mistranscription for the fiftieth psalm?).

'our prinicipal founder', and Nicholas de Baskerville, 'who gave us an annual rent of 26s 8d'.[48]

At Vyšší Brod several members of the dynasty of Wok von Rosenberg find mention, some of whom held high positions in the kingdom of Bohemia, as Wok himself who founded the abbey in 1262, was marshal of the kingdom, and died seven years later. His entry in the necrology is accompanied by the words: 'vivat, vivat, in aeternum'.[49] Wok was buried in the choir, in what was later noted as the 'tomb of the founders'.

Wok's grandson, Peter, when his marriage to Viola came to an end in 1317 with her early death, gave to the abbey the vill of Eybensteyn, worth 80 pounds. In 1322, on the death of his uncle, John of Dobruska, Peter gave the monastery fifty sexagenas for the purchase of clothing, and a further fifty for a pittance. In 1346, his son Bartholomew gave the monastery sixty-seven sexagenas. His nephew, Henry of Plumnan, who died in 1344, gave one hundred sexagenas 'from which we purchased the vill of Swynyehlawa'. Henry von Rosenberg gave many gifts, including 'a gold ornamented cross, and a monstrance with precious stones'. More than that, he obtained from Boniface IX in 1403 the abbot's right to wear pontificalia.[50]

---

[48] NCR, pp. 661–2; NNH, pp. 692–3.
[49] An essay on the relations between Wok and the Cistercian Order is to be found online: A. Wagner, *Wok von Rosenberg*, pp. 173–98.
[50] NHN, pp. 382–90.

Founders, Major Patrons and Benefactors

The English nunnery of Wintney could also boast two founders. Its necrology tells that the initial founder (in the late twelfth century) was Richard Holt, whose wife was Christina Cobreth. It also tells of a Dionisia Cobreth, 'whose heart lies buried before the high altar', not a very common occurrence in a Cistercian church. There follows notice of Richard of Herierde (*ob.* 1240), 'of pious memory, our benefactor, founder of our stone church'.[51]

Tintern abbey (W) was founded in 1131 by Walter de Clare, Lord of Chepstow, but the new impressive church, funded by Roger Bigod, Earl of Norfolk and now lord of Chepstow, and mostly complete by 1288, led to Bigod also being described as 'founder' in the monastery's *obit* book, and to his arms being glazed on the new east window.

The monks of Oliwa (P) saw Sobiesław I, duke of Pomerania (*ob.* 1178), as their first founder, and Duke Sambor I (*ob.* 1207), as their second founder, but they also acknowleged as a 'founder' Duke Swantopolk II, who died in 1266.[52]

An obituary might also mention the origins of the community. We learn that in 1184, led by Abbot Peter I, monks came from Trois-fontaines (F) to found Szent Gotthard (Hg). He died that autumn. As for the nunnery of Baindt (G), its necrology tells how on 3 January 1241, 'This [place] became God's house

---

[51] *NWN*, pp. 387–8, 391: a reminder that early Cistercian churches were often of timber.
[52] *NTN*, p. 268; *NOL*, pp. 505–7.

with great solemnity';[53] it adds, the purport is not clear, of 20 May, that 'This is a day of remembrance, a day of favour for God's house', meaning the abbey.[54] Kołbacz (P) was the founding house of Oliwa, and its abbot Goswin gave its daughter monastery one hundred Slavonic marks. The necrology of Orval (B), also a daughter-house of Trois-fontaines, tells of its own foundation in 1131, giving its official Latin name of 'Aurea Vallis'. The necrology of Neuzelle (G) tells how in 1147 Abbot Godeschalc came from Morimond with a community to found Heiligenkreuz (A).[55]

Nor were patrons forgotten, as at Ląd (P), with its remembrance of King John Sobieski III of Poland, 'protector of our Order', who died in 1697. The necrology of Sorø (D) tells of the death on 28 February, though no year is given, of 'Prince John, illustrious king of the Danes, and especial benefactor of our Order'.[56] That of Lilienfeld (A) remembered King Ladislas of Hungary and Bohemia, and Duke of Austria, as its 'special friend'. The necrology of Wilhering (A) told of King Frederick III of the Romans as being a major benefactor. That of Orval, in remembering its many grantors, told that on each day of their *obits*, the seven penitential psalms should be recited. The

---

[53] NHG; NBT, p. 232.
[54] NHG; NBT, pp. 232, 237; a term also used by the nuns of Lilienthal: NTK, *passim*.
[55] NOL, p. 507; NO, p. 227; NNC, n.p.
[56] NLA, p. 487; NSR, p. 578. This was King John, who ruled from 1481 to 1513.

necrology of Heiligenkreuz spelt out in detail that on 12 January 1519, King Maximilian I had died 'at the third hour after the middle of the night'.[57]

MONETARY AND OTHER DONATIONS

Apart from receving lands and other assets from benefactors, many a monastery profited from outright gifts in cash, difficult now to equate to modern values. One pound sterling in the year 1400 is reckoned to be equivalent to £600 today, and the like in 1600 would be around £140 now. In the fourteenth and fifteenth centuries the Rhenish coinage (florin) was minted in Cologne, Mainz and Triest, and was then in wide circulation.[58]

Fortunate was Port-Royal (F), where monetary grants and annuities made by thirty-three individuals totalled over 900 Paris pounds, over 900 Tournai pounds and a further 140 unspecified pounds, including generous grants by French queens. Lack of early documentation must mean that these figures are only a fraction of the true total. Port-Royal was also well served by its thirteenth abbess, Agnès de Trier (*ob. c.*1348), 'who raised a thousand pounds for the restoration of the monastery, cloister and

---

[57] *NW*, p. 130. This was Frederick III, who died in 1493; *NO, passim, NH*, p. 112.

[58] I am extremly grateful to Mrs Fran Stroobarts, Head of Coins and Medals, the Royal Library of Belgium, for this information.

houses'.[59] The several benefactors of Maubuisson (F) gave in total to the convent by direct gift, or in rents, or in bequests, a known total of around 4,000 pounds; again perhaps a fraction of its actual receipts. A lesser nunnery was Notre-Dame-des-Prés (F), but it was able to list amongst its benefactors who gave it lands an archdeacon, a canon and a knight.[60]

Amongst known benefactions were those from individuals connected to a monastery, as at Bronnbach (G), where Blaesius Düenbach (*ob.* 1611), a servant, 'left to the church twenty florins', and its cook, John Hammer (*ob.* 1657), left fifty florins, whilst Oliwa (P) benefited from a gift of 200 florins each from Felix and Euphrasyna, brother and sister-in-law of Abbot Konarsky. Local prelates might assist, such as Bishop Francis Kusmalcz of Warmia, who gave Pelplin (P) in 1457, 'at the time of discord in the province, eighty pounds of good money': it was the year of the death of Wartislas IX, duke of Pomerania. Many were as generous as they could afford to be, like John Leo, a canon of Godestad, Sweden (*ob.* 1635), who left Pelplin 1,000 Prussian marks.[61]

More than one benefactor of Soleilmont desired 'an annual *obit* for his father and mother, brothers and sisters'. This was a frequent request, such as that made by King Frederick of the Romans (*ob.* 1493), who gave Feldbach (G) thirty marks in return 'for

---

[59] NPR, *passim*, and p. 639.
[60] NM, *passim*; NDP, ff. 5r, 6d.
[61] NBR, pp. 105, 98; NOL, pp. 525, 534; NPL, pp. 67, 77.

Monetary and Other Donations

a daily Mass to be celebrated in perpetuity'.[62] Two sections of the cartulary of Fontenelle (F) list benefactors who had requested that their *obit* be kept with the sum of money they had donated. Amongst them were a chaplain of the Steward of Flanders remembered on 9 August against a bequest of fifteen shillings, and on 22 November a Madame Yde de Boviler was commemorated, having left twenty shillings. Of a major benefactor to Pairis (F), John Trut (*ob*. 1472), a canon of Colmar, its necrology notes that 'he ought to have, on 5 May, absolution after Vigils, and Mass at his tomb in the Chapel of the 1,000 Virgins, with cross, holy water and thurible'.[63]

A number of bequests specify 'all he had', or 'all she had', as in grants by John Sliwka to Jędrzejów (P), and by Agnes de Püch to Fürstenfeld (G). The value is often stated, as when Hans Scolze gave Pelplin (P) 'all his goods, in value 700 marks', or when Apollonia Bundschugin (*ob*. 1683), a widow, gave to Bronnbach (G) 'all her immovable goods in Reichholtzheim, valued at 2,000 florins'. It was noted at Lilienfeld (A) of Hainrich am Schayds, that 'he gave us all his goods before his death'.[64] At Pelplin (P) a familiar, its shoemaker, 'gave us all his goods', and at Heiligenkreuz (A), a novice, brother John, presumably dying young, did the same. For Wettingen (Sw)

---

[62] *NSO, passim*, but e.g. p. 410; *NFD*, p. 390.
[63] *CMF*, pp. 16–24, 99–104; *NPS*, p. 73.
[64] *NJD*, p. 803; *NFN*, p. 100; *NPL*, p. 73; *NLD*, p. 421.

Burkard of Egenwile not only provided drink for the community in Lent, 'but dying left us everything'.[65]

As time progressed religious were allowed 'pocket money': Martin Czubaich, a carpenter, gave 44 talents to Lilienfeld 'from which each of the convent receives one florin'. Goetrid Müller, giving silk cloth to Wettingen for making a chasuble, also gave 'to each monk four coins'.[66] Grants might help religious in other ways: Cistercian monks were bled quarterly, but at Aldersbach (G) it was for some reason a local cleric, Conrad, 'who procured for us the fourth day annually in bleeeding', whilst for Ebrach (G), as early as 1150, a grant of wine was made for those 'weakened when bled'.[67]

CHURCHES

The necrologies give little detail regarding the early monastic churches, but much consideration to their rebuilding and enhancements, though that of Neuzelle (G) tells of its first monastery in 1304 being a timber structure, to which monks came from Altzelle. There are to be found the undated names of *muratores* (lit. 'wall-builders'), such as Ulric (*ob.* 7 October) and Ulrich Smuczär ('murator in this church'; *ob.* 15 November) at Engelszell (A), Andrew at Rein (A;

---

[65] *NPL*, p. 74; *NH*, p. 117; *NWT*, p. 594.
[66] *NLD*, p. 386; *NWT*, p. 597.
[67] *NA*, p. 18 ('plebanus'); *NEBR*, p. 133.

fourteenth/fifteenth century), and Joseph George Adam Ginter (*ob.* 1789), a *conversus*, at Koronowo (P).[68]

Pelplin's 'builder', Peter Reis Helvetus, who died in 1623, left the church 'a substantial sum, in value more than 600 Polish florins'. Hainrich, a monk, was 'master of the works' at Bebenhausen (G) in the 1220s. A monk of Bornem (B), Vincent de Clercq (*ob.* 1836), played a major role in the restoration of his abbey from 1828.[69] As for church dedications, the necrology of Salem (A) points out that 'from antiquity' it had named, as its secondary patron, St Michael the Archangel, since with very few exceptions Cistercian churches were dedicated, like that of Lucelle, to 'Our Lady, Saint Mary'.[70]

In the building history of Salem, two abbots stood out: Peter Oxer, the fifteenth abbot, who died in 1441, and had 'completed the new structure of our church, and a new dorter, chapter-house and cloister', and Stephen Jung, the thirty-fifth abbot, who died in 1725, 'during whose rule the new building of this monastery was constructed after the burning of the monastery in the wars of the times'[71] (this may refer to the fire which consumed its buildings in 1697, though the church was spared then). As for Ebrach (G), in the early eighteenth century a new tower was made, 'completely covered in copper'. At Ląd (P),

[68] *NNC*, n.p.; *NE*, pp. 253, 255; *NRE*, p. 346; *NKN*, p. 150.
[69] *NPL*, p. 85; *NBE*, p. 263; *NBM*, p. 5.
[70] *NSL*, p. 251; *NLC*, p. 40.
[71] *NSL*, pp. 133 and 108, respectively.

Abbot Lukomski (*ob.* 1750) laid marble pavements and covered the towers with copper. A successor, Abbot Raczynski, covered most of the church in copper. At an unknown date, Nicholas Mylon, a priest and official in Gdańsk, gave Oliwa 'two lecterns in the middle of the choir made of fine copper'.[72]

At Zwettl (A) the necrology tells of the new choir erected around 1347, and in 1348 John of Chunring, 'our founder', died, 'and was buried in the new choir'. The next year so too was his brother, Leopold. In 1346, at Michaelmas, 'the renowned Ludwig of Öetting, a son-in-law of King Albert of the Romans' died. He was buried at Zwettl 'by the altar of the Holy Trinity, as the first stone laid in the new foundation'—presumably referring to his gravestone. The year 1347 saw the death of Ulrich, 'servant of the *custos*' (meaning official of the cellarer), 'who gave sixty talents, and lies at the altar in the new choir dedicated in honour of Ss Udalric and Leonard'. At this time, John of Paris, 'who died in our house at Vienna, gave 100 talents towards the construction of the new choir'. This period of joy was replaced nearly a century later, when it was noted that Abbot Frederick had died 'after 1424, and before the burning of the monastery'.[73]

Within a monastery church, the high altar was a focal point of great significance, and, as noted, burial close to it was a great privilege. The *obit* of

[72] *NEBR*, p. 106; *NLA*, pp. 485, 479, respectively; *NOL*, p. 530.
[73] *NZ*, pp. 570–1.

Churches

an unnamed duke of Bavaria at Lilienfeld was to be kept 'with a requiem at the high altar with sixteen candles', while of the same abbey its necrology notes that Ferdinand II, archduke of Austria (*ob.* 1595), 'liberally completed the high altar with sixteen candles'. A later abbot there, Chrysostom Wieser (*ob.* 1747), 'built a magnificent marble altar, and decorated the whole church wonderfully'. Following the baroque renovation of Neuzelle (G), Bishop Andrew Zaluski of Culm consecrated its new high altar in 1741. Cistercian simplicity was being lost![74]

Other gifts for a high altar included 'a sum of silver for the repair of the tabernacle' (Marche-les-Dames, B); 'a perpetual light before the Blessed Sacrament' (Marche-les-Dames); 'the light always burning before the Venerable Sacrament' (Kamieniec, P; 1615); 'a cross set about with precious stones' (Lilienfeld, A); 'an image of the Blessed Virgin Mary' (Newenham, E); and a gift in 1423 of twenty florins for adornment (Wettingen, Sw).[75]

Grants for the upkeep of monastic church buildings noted in the necrologies include 'lead for the work of the nave of our church' (Newminster, E), suggesting necessary roof repairs in 1429; 'thirty-one pounds to repair our roof' (given by Abbot William of Salem to Feldbach nunnery (Sw); 66 pounds of broken stone for the church (Notre-Dame-des-Près,

---

[74] *NLD*, p. 370; *NL*, pp. 46, 53; *NNC*, n.p.
[75] *NMD*, pp. 158, 156; *NKM*, image 18 (by 1615); *NNH*, p. 693; *NWT*, p. 589 (this in 1423).

F);[76] 200 florins, 'and twenty florins for the clock' (Wettingen, Sw; by the provost of Basle cathedral); thirty florins 'for making the Cross and images of Our Lady and St John in the choir, and for maintaining the Calvary, three bonniers' (Soleilmont, B); and 'a wooden statue of the Virgin seated on a silver plate borne by four angels, she holding a fleur-de-lis' (Maubuisson, given by Queen Jean of France and Navarre, *ob.* 1371).[77]

At an unknown date, a candelabra was presented to Pelplin (P) to stand before its image of Our Lady. A statue of Our Lady stood in the cloister at Cambron (B). During the abbacy of Abbot Henry IV of Ebrach (1437–47), a clock was affixed to its church. When, in 1464, the high altar at Lilienthal was refurbished at a cost of forty-six Rhenish guilders, its nuns were bidden yearly to give thanks by the chanting of the anthem 'I will exalt thee' in choir.[78]

ARTISTRY

Cistercian simplicity was increasingly lost with the adornment of monastic churches by the seventeenth century, and artistic members were to be found within Cistercian communities, and in especial painters, such as Albert, a monk of Ląd (P; *ob.* 1605); Joseph, a

---

[76] *NNM*, p. 401; *NFD*, p. 393; *NDP*, f. 5v.
[77] *NWT*, p. 592; *NSO*, p. 439; *NM*, p. 657.
[78] *NPL*, p. 87; *NC*, p. 133; *NEBR*, p. 201; *NTK*, p. 533.

monk of Vištytis (P; *ob.* 1785, aged 71); George Buck, a *conversus* of Salem (A, *ob.* 1673); Stephen Molitor (*ob.* 1695), a *conversus* of Heilgenkreuz; and Nicholas, a familiar of Pelplin (P).[79]

It was a layman artist who, at an unknown date, 'painted with his own hands the picture at the public altar' at Stams (A), but it was a monk of Langheim (G), John Sigler (*ob.* 1622), who painted there three ships on a blue field, with the words (in Latin): 'I pray you most holy and bountiful God, renowned Creator, that I be not ship-wrecked on the islands of the sea'. Amadeus Bernard (*ob.* 1708), a *conversus* of Aulps, was a sculptor. At Vyšší Brod (C) a *conversus*, Peregrine Pitter (*ob.* 1920), was 'sculptor and gilder'.[80]

WINDOWS

By the later fourteenth century the original simplicity of unadorned grisaille glass in monastic church windows began to give way to coloured glass. By 1387 stained glass at Zwettl (A) depicted, amongst others, Ss Benedict, Martin and John the Evangelist, as well as Peter and Paul. At unknown dates, Henneke Man gave Neuencamp (G) eighty marks for 'a better window in our church', and Heneke Kos gave the monastery 200 marks and, moreover, 'made a glass window in our church'. The necrology of Roermond

---

[79] *NLA*, p. 496; *NKN*, p. 88; *NSL*, p. 196; *NNC*, n.p; *NPL*, p. 89.
[80] *NST*, p. 54; *NLH*, p.292; *NAP*, p. 137; *NNC*, n.p.

lauded John of Dript, 'from whom we have a glass window in our choir'.

There are notes of new windows made in the cloisters at Engelszell (A) and Fürstenfeld (G),[81] but at uncertain dates. Some *conversi* are listed as glaziers: John at Ląd (*ob.* 1673), George Waldemann at Salem (A; *ob.* 1802), and Achatius Staus at Ebrach (G), 'who reglazed the whole church with new pictures', but sadly died of apoplexy in 1812.[82]

MUSIC

Regarding sacred music, some religious were noted as of special merit, such as Thaddeus at Ląd (P), only a deacon when he died in 1630; at Neuberg (A), a monk, John Lyndale (*ob.* 1603), 'a good musician'; and a jubilarian, Stephen Urany (*ob.* 1710), 'versed in Gregorian chant', and at Ebrach, Clement Faulstich (*ob.* 1783), 'rector of the choir'. In the sixteenth century a musician, Stanislas Lazowi, was a 'special servant of the house' at Jędrzejów (P).[83]

The position of cantor was crucial, and at Bronnbach (G) two sub-priors held this post in addition to their other duties: Conrad Breller (*ob.* 1530), and John Nonnepoeus (*ob.* 1630). A monk, Anthony (*ob.* 1584), was cantor at Aulps for twenty-eight years. At St-Ber-

---

[81] NZ, p. 571; NN, p. 510; NE, p. 244; NFN, p. 103.
[82] NLA, p. 484; NRM, p. 47; NSL, p. 250; NEBR, p. 306.
[83] NLA, p. 496; NNB, p. 34; NNB, p. 38; NEBR, p 295; NJD, p. 804.

Music

nard-sur-l'Escaut (B) Nicholas Peter (*ob.* 1452), monk, once held the position. Amongst the *cantrices* of Seligenthal nunnery (G) were Chûnigund Ebranin and Ellgeb Tûnczin; for each, as with some other entries, their necrology expresses the hope that 'she may have everlasting life, Amen'.[84]

At Salem (A) there was a strong musical tradition by the time of its early monk-organists, John Hug (*ob.* 1451), also a painter and scribe, and George Ruthart (*ob.* 1496). Three later monks were both cantor and organist, and Ambrose Rothmund (*ob.* 1751) was the choir master. Sebastian Schauber (*ob.* 1814) was a composer and music teacher; and John Augustan (*ob.* 1814) was a music professor. One of Salem's jubilarians, Thaddeus Weitmann (*ob.* 1806), had been 'for many years instructor of music for the juniors'; whilst another, Arnulph Tribelhorn, was 'a player of the flute'. At St Urban (Sw), Rudolph Mohr (*ob.* 1864) was noted as a 'tenor in the choir'.[85]

At an unknown date, a lay musician, Jacob Klonski, gave to Jędrzejów (P) 150 florins and musical instruments. The church instrument which came to the fore by the later medieval period was the organ, which could be an expensive commodity; so at Ląd (P) a *conversus*, Nicholas (*ob.* 1647), built the abbey organ himself, whilst Neuencamp (G) received a gift of ninety marks with which to purchase an organ.[86]

---

[84] *NBR*, p. 113; *NBR*, p. 131; *NAP*, p. 131; *NBM*, p. 60; *NS*, passim.
[85] *NSL*, pp. 324, 133, 165, 134, 248–9, 221, 224.
[86] *NJD*, p. 498; *NLA*, p. 473; *NN*, p. 512.

A new organ had been installed at Ebrach (G) in 1745, and by 1773 the abbey had two organs, one in the choir, the other 'in the middle of the church'. At unknown dates, Catharine van den Bongart bequeathed gold, and Theodrica de Eyll money, to the nuns of Roermond, so their organ could be repaired.[87]

The necrologies include mentions of organists: monks, such as Theodore (*ob.* 1596) at Mogiła (P); Adam (*ob.* 1629) at Wągrowiec (P); Thomas (*ob.* 1483) at Raitenhaslach (G); and Amadeus Zoller of Salem (A; *ob.* 1750)—said to be 'an organist of great merit'; or familiars, such as Ludovic at Kamieniec (P; *ob.* 1525), where, at an unrecorded date, a *conversus*, Elias Beiterds, also played the organ.[88]

There are also frequent mentions of lay organists, such as George Kral, 'organist and faithful servant', at Kamieniec in the early seventeenth century; John Piotrowski (*ob.* 1618) and Joseph Zelaskowicz (*ob.* 1660) at Ląd (P); and Peter of Endovia, 'faithful minister of the church and organist' at Roermond. As for the choristers, three 'leaders of the choir' at Neuberg (A) died between 1772 and 1773, perhaps from an infectious disease?[89]

---

[87] *NEBR*, pp. 258, 290; *NRM*, pp. 74, 111.
[88] *NN*, p. 512; *NSL*, p. 6; *NKM*, p. 36; *NKM*, p. 23.
[89] *NKM*, image 54; *NLA*, pp. 488, 499; *NRM*, p. 36; *NNB*, p. 41.

VESTMENTS AND SACRED UTENSILS

Some vestments will have been made in-house by *conversi* tailors, but the necrologies tell of vestments also being presented as gifts. Lilienfeld (A), at an unknown date, received a cope and mitre (for the abbot), as well as two tunicles (the vestment of subdeacons). Mary of Flanders, Abbess of Solières (B), presented the nuns of Marche-les-Dames (B), where she had been professed, with a chasuble and two dalmatics (the vesture of a deacon). A nun there gave, perhaps on her profession, two green dalmatics.[90]

Abbot Bruno Cloquette of Villers (B; abbot 1788–1828), gave 'the noble nuns' of Hocht, where in a time of political trouble he had taken refuge, 'a splendid damask chasuble'. The necrology of Roermond notes the gifts of several chasubles, black, green and damask, to its nuns, including one of green silk, given by Countess Maria de Bourbon, and adorned with the armorial insignia of herself and her husband. With the chasubles came the necessary appurtenances, 'stole, maniple and alb'.[91]

The lay tailor of Pelplin (P) gave that abbey 'a black chasuble for the altar of the dead'. Others might give the necessary cloth: for Wettingen (Sw), Goetfrid Müller gave 'silk cloth for making a chasuble', while the same nunnery received a gift of twenty florins

---

[90] *NV*, p. 86; *NRM*, pp. 20, 39, 55, 60–1.
[91] *NNB*, p. 41; *NL*, p. 30; *NLD*, p. 370; *NMD*, pp. 184, 195.

'for vestments'.[92] Vestments were the purview of the sacristan, such as Hermann Hermann (*ob.* 1771), a *conversus*, and 'very diligent servant of the sacristry' at Salem; John of Antwerp (*ob.* 1532) at St-Bernard-sur-l'Escaut (B); George Leysfriedt (*ob.* 1620), priest and sacristan at Neuberg; and Alexius, monk and sacrist at Kamieniec in 1702.[93]

Chalices were a frequent gift to a monastery, as noted in the necrologies of Fürstenfeld (G; 'for the altar of St Jerome'); Lilienfeld (two silver gilt chalices, *c.*1620); Mogiła (P; with a gift of forty marks); Preuilly (F; four silver chalices, *c.* 1207); and Wettingen (Sw; two chalices, 'one for the high altar, the other for the altar of St Peter').[94] From the later Midde Ages monstrances appear as a gift, as to Kaisheim (G; 'for the service of the Lord'); Neuberg (of silver, made in the abbey by a sixteenth-century monk); and Jędrzejów (P; together with a thurible, in return for 'one Mass of the Blessed Virgin Mary in the week').[95]

Amongst other necessities were indeed thuribles— Catherine, sister of Abbot James, gave Baudeloo (B) a silver thurible; John Codde (*ob.* 1709) gave it two silver candlesticks for the acolytes; for Fürstenfeld (G), Henry, a monk, 'wrote all the missal books of this house'. Preuilly (F) received 'a large gilt cross

---

[92] NV, p. 86; NPL, p. 112; NWT, pp. 597, 591.
[93] NSL, p. 221; NBM, p. p. 123; NNB, p. 35; NKM, image 63.
[94] NFN, p. 98; [NL, 61; NLD p. 380]; NML, p. 807; NP, p. 885; NWT, p. 590.
[95] NKH, p. 91; NNB, p. 34; NJD, p. 772. .

The calendar

with precious stones', and Jardin (F) a silver cross.[96] These were but a few of many gifts.

THE CALENDAR

Several necrologies relate the various feasts of the Church's year, with modifications appropriate for the Cistercian Order. There is more mention of octaves than is common today, as the 'octave of the Epiphany' at Salem (A), the octave of the Visitation (9 July) at Pelplin (P), the octave of St Bernard also at Pelplin (27 August), and at Zwettl (A; in 1408). Those of St Andrew (7 December), and of the Conception of Our Lady were observed at Baudeloo, and of her Assumption at Billigheim (G).[97] There is reference to perhaps long-forgotten feasts, such as that of the Crown of Thorns, kept on 11 August at Baudeloo, Billigheim (G), Rein (A) and Zwettl.[98]

The obituary of Lilienfeld (A) tells us that 'on the day of Corpus Christi all monks ought to carry lighted candles in the procession'. Alas! at Salem in 1732 one of its monks, Nivard Lempennbach, collapsed and died during the Corpus Christi procession. The necrology of Salem insisted that 'every year on the fifth feria after Ash Wednesday is celebrated with solemn office and four candles the anniversary of the illustrious

---

[96] *NB*, f. 13v (bis); *NFN*, p. 100; *NP*, p. 885; *NJ*, p. 431.
[97] *NSL*, p. 3; *NPL*, pp. 103, 95; *NZ*, p. 570; *NBH*, p. 63; *NB*, f. 42v.
[98] *NB*, f. 36v; *NBH*, p. 63; *NRE*, p. 349; *NZ*, p. 570.

archduke Albert of Austria'; there were several of that name. At some stage the abbey transferred its feast of dedication from the Sunday next to the feast of St Mary Magdalene to 16 July.[99] In north-west Europe, as at Baudeloo and Billigheim, the feast of St Thomas of Canterbury was frequently observed on 29 December. The monks of Val-St-Lambert remembered both Blessed Hugh of Cluny and Blessed Malachy, noting that he died at Clairvaux.[100]

COMMEMORATIONS

The purpose of a necrology was to list the dates of death of all those whose *obit* should be remembered; the day of month is invariably given, less so the year of death. Certain general commemorations were common to the Order as whole, such as the Commemoration of Departed Bishops and Abbots of the Order each 11 January.[101] A commemoration throughout the Order was also kept of all departed monks and nuns; at Fürstenzell (G) and Rein and Wilhering (A), this was observed on 20 May, but on 21 May at Baudeloo.[102]

---

[99] [NL, p. 89; NLD, p. 390]; NSL, p. 165; NSL, pp. 71, 249.
[100] NB, p. 29, and as a feast of Twelve Lessons; NBH, p. 66; NBL, p. 329: the Necrology of Boulancourt records 'T. archbishop of Canterbury', on 28 February; NSLB, ff. 28r, 71r.
[101] E.g. NC, p. 178; NM, p. 654; NSA, p. 475; NST, p. 48; NPS, p. 62, where the commemoration was transferable if 11 November happened to be a Sunday.
[102] NF, p. 114; NRE, p. 347; NW, p. 92; NB, f. 26v.

Commemorations

The date of commemoration of founders varied: 31 July at Maulbronn (G), 8 November at Bronnbach (G) and 12 December at Pairis (F).[103] There were many individual references to founders and benefactors (as noted above), such as Mestwin II (*ob.* 1255), recorded at Pelplin (P) as the 'founder of new Doberan (G)', and at Soleilmont (B), Monsieur de Fontaine and his wife (*ob.* 1610), who bequeathed 105 florins expecting its prayers.[104]

Foremost in the thoughts of many religious may have been their families back home, those who had nurtured the now professed monks and nuns. On 20 November, the Order therefore kept, as the necrology of Jardin (F) put it: 'the commemoration of fathers, mothers, brothers, sisters and parents'; if 20 November happened to be a Sunday, the observance was transferred to the next day.[105]

The necrology of the nunnery of Wintney (E) had the date of 21 October wrongly listed for this commemoration, but its remembrance that day was wide-ranging: 'of our fathers, mothers, brothers, sisters, all blood relations, and all deceased brothers and sisters and benefactors of our Order'. Similar wording was employed in many of the individual *obits* observed at Stams (A). At La Cour-Dieu (F)

---

[103] *NPS1*, p. 60; *NBR*, p. 137; *NPS*, p. 93.
[104] *NPL*, p. 122; *SEO*, p. 399, respectively.
[105] *NJ*, p. 433; *Cf. NPL*, p. 177, NR, p. 281; *NBH*, p. 65 — where 21 November given, and *NB*, f. 49r — where the 18th; at Rein: 'fathers, mothers, brothers, sisters, and blood relatives': *NRE*, p. 354.

on 20 November the departed religious of over a hundred other monastic communities were also remembered.[106]

The numbers of names of family members remembered could be considerable: the 'book of the dead' of Kamieniec (P) listed no fewer than nine hundred. The necrology of Marche-les-Dames (B) named over five hundred relatives of the community granted an annual *obit*.[107] Parents of an abbot might be remembered, as Ottilia (*ob.* 1406) and Mutteter, father and mother of Abbot John of Tennenbach (G), or the brothers of a monk, such as Nicholas, Paul and Jacob, brothers of John of Wąchock (P); or the sister of a monk, such as Barbara (*ob.* 1715), sister of Alberic, monk of Kamieniec (P); or the uncle of a nun, as Rotard, uncle of Margaret, nun of St Servaas.[108]

The Kamieniec obituary noted Anna (*ob.* 1612), mother of Jacob, *conversus*, and of Michael, father of Michael and Margareth, familiars. At Stams (A) individual *obits* were sometimes accompanied by words such as: 'And their forebears, children and their children, living and dead'. At Val-St-Lambert (B), it was hoped that Henry and Ida, parents of a monk, John Hazeek, 'may rest in peace. Amen'.[109]

Monastic obituaries included the departed religious of other monasteries, especially those tied to them in kinship. The necrology of Lilienfeld (A)

---

[106] NWN, p. 392; NST, *passim*; NCD, pp. 78–180.
[107] NKM, *passim*; NMD, *passim*.
[108] NT, p. 340; NJD, p. 773; NKM, image 2; NSS, p. 169.
[109] NKM, images 11, 34; NST, *passim*; NSLB, f. 12v.

refers to the *obits* of religious of Heiligenkreuz (A; its mother-house), and also to those of Zwettl (A). The necrology of Altzelle (G) makes frequent reference to the *obits* of abbots, monks and *conversi* of Pforta (G), its mother-house; so also of Walkenried (G), the mother-house of Pforta, with some references to *obits* of religious of Lubiąż (P), also a daughter-house of Pforta, as well as to the departed religious of Ebrach (G), and of Grâce-Dieu in France-Comté, both, like Altzelle, of the lineage of Morimond.[110]

The obituary of Neuencamp notes the *obits* of Abbot Andrew of Camp (G), and of Hermann, once abbot of Hiddensee (G), a monastery founded on an island given it by Neuencamp. The necrology of Vauluisant records the *obits* of its first abbot, Norpaud (*ob.* 1159), and of the first abbot of Preuilly, Artald, its mother-house. The necrology of Seligenthal nunnery (G) includes the *obit* of Leonard Eschellbacher (*ob.* 1486), prior of Raitenhaslach, a monastery with which the nuns had close contact. On 25 January each year the sisters remembered 'our priests and brothers in Raitenhaslach'.[111]

Billigheim remembered 'Hernand, our dearly beloved father, once prior in Bronnbach'; the nuns of Soleilmont remembered Hubert, 'worthy abbot of Florennes'. The monks of Salem listed one of their number who became the first abbot of Raitenhaslach, a daughter-house: Blessed Gero Auer von

---

[110] NLD, NAZ, *passim*.
[111] NN, pp. 517, 514; NVL, p. 55; NSA, pp. 476, 478.

Grasbeuren (*ob.* 1153); whilst the monks of Kamieniec kept an *obit* for eight early deceased nuns of Trzebnica.[112]

The monks of Engelszell (A) remembered Abbot Hainrich of Wilhering (there were four of that name), and Sorø (D) Abbot Laurence of Herrivad. At Cambron were kept the *obits* of both Abbot John of Foigny (*ob.* 1483) and Archbishop Baldwin of Canterbury, once abbot of Ford (E), who died at Acre in 1190; his *obit* was also kept at La Cour-Dieu. The nuns of Wald remembered King Richard on 'the third feria after the octave of Easter'.[113]

The lower ranks were not ignored. At Port-Royal was kept the *obit* of Robert de Thumery (*ob.* 1560/68), prior of Vaux-de-Cernay; at Kamieniec that of Peter Pictserkins (*ob.* 1627), monk of Henryków; at Rein, that of Chunrad, a *conversus* of Ebrach, and at Moulins, that of Jehanne Labatz (*ob.* 1643), a *conversa* of La Ramée. The obituary of Orval (B) calls to mind the *obit* of Fleur, a béguine. At Val-St-Lambert (B) the *obits* were noted of Theodoric, dean of St Lambert in Liège, and of John Huber, dean of the church there of St Dionysius.[114]

---

[112] *NBH*, p. 66; *NSO*, p. 424; *NBH*, p. 61; *NSL*, p. 135; *NKM*, image 24.
[113] *NE*, p. 250; *NSR*, p. 583; *NC*, pp. 113, 232; *NCD*, p. 173; *NWD*, p. 219.
[114] *NPRL2*, p. 638; *NKM*, image 13; *NRE*, 347; *NMS*, p. 502. *NO*, p. 228; *NLSB*, ff. 60r, 78r.

SHRINES

The necrology of Jędrzejów (P) tells of the tomb there of Blessed Wincenty (Vincent) Kadłubek, Bishop of Kraków until his death in 1223. The prior of the abbey, Jacob Voivodzki, who died aged ninety-eight in 1561, 'wrote many works in his praise'. In the 1640s his grave became a shrine as Benedict, a *conversus* of the monastery who died in 1647, had 'by his work and effort translated the bones of Blessed Vincent from a humble place into a marble mausoleum'. Count Wenzel of Opperstorff (*ob.* 1644) gave 'a golden chain and a lamp to adorn the mausoleum'.[115]

Abbot Henriou of Villers erected in 1613 on a hill top 'the chapel of the Blessed Virgin of Monte Acuto', Clement VIII granting a plenary indulgence to pilgrims who prayed there on the feasts of St Arnolph (18 July) and St Julian (27 January). The abbot also 'translated the bodies of the saints concealed then behind the high altar and replaced them in an honoured place under a marble sarcophagus in the chapel of St Bernard'.[116]

RELICS

Pride of place in any abbey was a portion of the True Cross, such as, its necrology tells us, Leopold

---

[115] *NJD*, pp. 778, 792, 804–5.
[116] *NV*, p. 54.

the Virtuous, 5th duke of Austria (*ob*. 1194), brought back with him from the Holy Land, and gave to Heiligenkreuz (A). Zawiss de Falkensteyn (*ob*. 1290) gave Vyšší Brod (C) 'the sacred wood of the Cross of the Lord, ornamented with precious stones', whilst Katherine, widow of Peter of Rosenberg, gave the house a gold chalice (decorated with the hair of St Mary Magdalene) and a monstrance (set with a tooth of St Benedict).[117] Wolfgang of Stubenerg, buried at Rein (A), gave it a relic of the Holy Cross, and of the brain of St Andrew. Pelplin (P), too, had a relic of the Holy Cross, whilst Archbishop William of Rouen (*ob*. 1306) gave Maubuisson (F) relics of St Paul and St Catherine.[118]

The obituary of Pairis nunnery (F) relates that it kept the day of St Thecla, Virgin and Martyr, on 23 September, as a Feast of Twelve Lessons, because 'her severed head is with us'. Doubt would be cast today on the veracity of some of these relics. The necrology of Vauluisant (F) tells that on the feast of the Annunication (25 March) in 1517, its monks placed the head of St Theodore, martyr, in a new reliquary. Abbess Phelippe of Port-Royal (F; *ob*. 1291) gave her nuns 'a cross and reliquary of silver, and a golden pyx for the Blessed Sacrament'.[119]

---

[117] *NH*, p. 120; *NNC*, n.p; *NHN*, pp. 383, 386.
[118] *NRE*, p. 353; *NPL*, p. 67; *NM*, p. 656.
[119] *NPS*, p. 85; *NVL*, p. 54; *NPR*, pp. 644–5.

Subsidiary Altars

SUBSIDIARY ALTARS

Before the close of the twelfth century, it became increasingly the practice for each monk to offer a daily private Mass. This necessitated the construction of several subsidiary altars within an abbey church, perhaps in an apse, in the transepts, the cloister, the chapter-house, or elsewhere.[120] The several necrologies bear abundant witness to their presence. No less than twelve altars are noted at Fürstenfeld (G), dedicated to the Holy Spirit, Saints Bartholomew, Catherine, George (in the cloister), Gregory, Philip and James, Jerome, John the Evangelist, Peter and Paul, Simon and Jude and Stephen.[121]

The record of Lilienfeld (A) tells of at least nine subsidiary altars: of the Holy Cross, the Holy Trinity (at the gate), and Ss Andrew, Benedict, Caesarius, Gregory, John the Evangelist, Margaret and Wolfgang (this in the chapter-house). By 1345 Aldersbach (G) also had an altar in its chapter-house. By the close of the eighteenth century, Ebrach (G) had fifteen altars of alabaster; nine of which were embellished with paintings of images, such as Jesus, Mary and Joseph, Peter the Penitent and Christ upon the Cross.[122]

There were few side-altars dedicated to Our Lady, as most Cistercian churches had her patronage,

---

[120] See also David. H. Williams, *The Cistercians in the Early Middle Ages*, 1998, p. 225.
[121] *NFN, passim.*
[122] *NA*, p. 20; *NLD, passim*; *NEBR*, pp. 302, 323.

though they are noted at Cambron (B) and Villers (B), and one in honour of the Assumption at Rein, whilst the necrology of Salem (A) noted that 'on the Sunday next after the octave of the Epiphany, after the first office, the Mass of the Dedication of the chapel of the Virgin Mary is sung solemnly with processional Vespers'.[123]

A popular dedication was to the Holy Cross, as at Raitenhaslach (G), before which altar in 1416 Albrecht and Friederich, the eldest sons of Duke Henry XVI of Bavaria, were laid to rest.[124] The Austrian abbeys at Engelszell (placed in the cloister), Heiligenkreuz, Lilienfeld, Stams, Wettingen and Jędrzejów (P), were amongst many with an altar so dedicated. At Zwettl (A), Friderich Gnemhertl, 'faithful friend of all religious', was buried in 1339 'before the altar of the Holy Cross, but his wife close to the altar of St Andrew'.[125]

Other frequent dedications included those of the Holy Trinity, as at Croxden, Engelszell, Koronowo, Rein, Wettingen and Wilhering;[126] of St Andrew, as at Lilienfeld, Rein and Zwettl;[127] of St Stephen, as at Bronnbach (G), Cambron (B), Fürstenzell (G), Seligenthal (G) and Pairis (F);[128] and of St John the

---

[123] *NC*, p. 108; *NV*, p. 52; *NRE*, p. 348; *NSL*, p. 3 ('ambabus').
[124] *NR*, pp. 260, 270;
[125] *NE*, p. 243; *NH*, p. 109; *NL*, p. 103; *NST*, p. 55; *NWT*, p. 598; *NJD*, p. 805; *NZ*, p. 570.
[126] *NCR*, p. 661; *NE*, p. 250; *NKN*, p. 155; *NRE*, p. 348; *NWT*, p. 589; *NWL*, p. 455.
[127] *NLD*, p. 501; *NRE*, p. 346; *NZ*, 570.
[128] *NBR*, p. 108; *NC*, pp. 108, 133; *NFN*, p. 100; *NSA*, p. 482; *NPS*, p. 71.

Burials and Sepulchral Monuments

Baptist, as at Aldersbach, Engelszell, Heiligenkreuz and Rein.[129]

Cambron had a chapel of St Engelbert, and Lilienfeld an altar of St Wolfgang in its chapter-house. Werner, an imperial procurator, gave Fürstenfeld (G) 500 florins for a perpetual Mass at its altar of Ss Philip and James, whilst two ladies endowed a light at its altar of St Gregory, 'where they are buried'. Lilienfeld received a silver cross for St Benedict's altar, and support for a lamp at its altar of St Margaret.[130]

Two benefactors of Aldersbach provided for two Masses in the week at its altars of St James and St Peter. The Trinity chapel at Wettingen 'was constructed from his own resources' by a local cleric, Hartlieb (*ob.* 1274), 'together with all utensils necessary and a burning light'. The necrology of Salem (A) notes that in 1619 the General Chapter reduced the number of lamps in a monastic church to five, but in 1741 Abbot Anselm II added a sixth lamp there.[131]

BURIALS AND SEPULCHRAL MONUMENTS

As noted above, founders, their families and major benefactors frequently had the privilege of being laid to rest 'in the choir', and thus 'before the high altar'. Others to have this honour included Philip Bischoff,

---

[129] *NA*, p. 16; *NE*, p. 246; *NH*, p.111; *NRE*, p. 343.
[130] *NC*, p. 101; *NFN*, pp. 100, 98; *NLD*, pp. 376, 411, 423.
[131] *NA*, pp. 21, 25; *NWT*, p.594.; *NSL*, pp. 4, 283.

proconsul of Gdańsk (*ob.* 1482), 'at the presbytery step' in Oliwa (P); Bishop Chunrad of Frisia (*ob.* 1340) 'before the high altar' at Lilienfeld, he having done 'much good' for the monastery; and Bishop Ansellus of Laon (*ob.* 1238) at Vauluisant (F). In 1386 Otto, margrave of Hachberg, was killed in conflict, and was interred at Tennenbach (G) 'before the great altar'.[132]

Interment in the chapter-house was primarily the perquisite of deceased abbots, such as Thomas, the first abbot of Croxden (E; *ob.* 1229); at Tennenbach (G), John Lepus (*ob.* 1396), its thirteenth abbot, and its seventeenth abbot, Nicholas Rieftlin (*ob.* 1449), to name but a few.[133] In Austria four early dukes were interred in the chapter-house of Heiligenkreuz: Leopold I in 1141; Leopold II on Christmas Eve 1193, vested 'in monastic habit'; Leopold V, in 1194, by whom was laid to rest Frederick I, who died at Acre in 1198 on his way home from the Crusades, as well as in 1137 eighteen-year-old Ernst, 'son of our founder'. Other nobility of the Babenburg family, stretching from Prince Friederich I (*ob.* 1198) to Friederich II (*ob.* 1246), also found their last resting place there.[134]

More than thirty members of the founding family were buried at Lucelle (Lützel; F), including, in the chapter-house, Albert of Habsurg, Landgrave of Alsatia. At Du Val (F), Margaret, lady of Marfontaun,

---

[132] *NOL*, p. 521; *NL*, p. 73; *NVL*, p. 55; *NT*, p. 341.
[133] *NCR*, p. 661 *NT*, pp. 340–1.
[134] *NH*, pp. 112–20.

was not the only female interred in its chapter-house, whilst Kunegund, noble lady of Tengen, was buried in the chapter-house at Wettingen (Sw). At Stams (A), John Bach, rector of Wertach, 'intimate patron and friend of us all', was buried 'at the entrance to the chapter-house'.[135]

As space in a chapter-house became exhausted, two deceased abbots might share the same grave, as Abbot Otto Grill (*ob.* 1362) and Abbot Ulrich Offerl (*ob.* 1408) did at Zwettl (A), the gravestone of the former being engraved with a pastoral staff. Shortage of space might mean abbots being laid to rest elsewhere, such as Abbot Peter of Ebrach (G; *ob.* 1404), 'a man of excellent determination, with a fruitful rule of nineteen years', who was interred at 'the sepulchre of the abbots, close to the door of the sacristy', although a later abbot of Ebrach, John (*ob.* 1533), was buried 'on the epistle side of the altar of St John the Evangelist', and 'his epitaph was affixed by a stone in the wall by the place of the Holy Cross'.[136]

In 1697 the remains of the first abbot of Ebrach, Blessed Adam (1126–61), were removed to a position also close to the door of the sacristy, where he was given a marble tomb, 'made as a square in ancient form'. Abbot Oliver of Pairis (*ob.* 1692), had to be buried 'by the presbytery step on the gospel side'. The secularisation of Salem in 1803 meant that its fortieth and last abbot, Caspar Oexle, dying in 1820,

---

[135] *NLC*, p. 41; *NVA*, p. 630; *NWT*, p. 590; *NST*, p. 52.
[136] *NZ*, p. 570; *NEBR*, pp. 196, 209.

was buried there 'before the high altar on the epistle side, only by the special grace of Archduke Ludovic'.[137]

Burials took place at Hauterive (Sw) in a variety of locations: a few abbots of the seventeenth and eighteenth centuries were interred 'in the presbytery before the tomb of the founder', or at the presbytery step, one 'at the middle step'; at least one other was laid to rest behind the abbot's stall. Burials of religious took place in the 'voids' before chapels dedicated to St John, St Anne, St Nicholas ('of Attalens') and the Annunciation; others, including some *conversi*, were laid to rest near the chapter-house, or 'in the void before the chapter-house'.[138]

Most monks were buried in the cloisters. Again space was a consideration, and when at Bronnbach (G) in 1710 two monks died, Philip Aysele, aged sixty-four, and Joseph Hoffman, just twenty-six, they were buried in the same tomb. When John Benicius, monk and confessor in the monastery, died at Langheim (G) in 1610, he was buried 'before the abbot's seat in the cloister'; dying in 1618, a later confessor, Zacharias Huepper, lay next to him. Two brothers, both canons of Colmar, dying in 1419 were buried together at Pairis (F) in the chapel of the 11,000 Virgins.[139]

---

[137] *NEBR*, pp. 130; *NPS*, p. 71; *NSL*, p. 167.
[138] *NHR, passim*; 'fossa' = ? 'void'. The restored chapel of St Nicholas, dating from 1320, is still in use today: C. Waeber, *Die zisterzienserabtei Hauterive*, Berne, 2009, pp. 37–8 (illus.).
[139] *NLH*, p. 290; *NKM*, image 40.

Burials and Sepulchral Monuments

When Chrisopher Bannach died at Langheim in 1625, he 'obtained the first place of burial in the new chapel of the dead'. Dying at Kamieniec (P) in 1712, Christian Stiller, a monk of Zbraslav (Bohemia), was buried there 'in the cloister amongst our brethren'. In the church of Koronowo (P), Marianna Charszewska, mother of Kilian, one of its monks, was interred in 1778.[140] At Cambron (B) six interments are noted in the choir and forty-one in the cloister. Interestingly, the footnotes of its necrology recount that each grave in the cloister had an allotted number, e.g. Place 1 (Nicholas Laurent, *ob.* 1641), or Place 22 (Augustine Bourdier, *ob.* 1609).[141]

The necrology of Pairis records forty-eight lay burials in its cloister, mostly in the first half of the fourteenth century, and in the same period some twenty-five lay burials 'in the church of the *conversi*' —namely the nave. These included in 1324 that of Hedwig, wife of Sigfrid, and in 1332, John Vro. At Bronnbach, a counsellor of the abbey, Joseph Bauermüller, dying in 1776, was interred 'in the middlle of the church, close to the altar of Ss Stephen and John'. At St Servaas, Utrecht, Henry Weg and Eef, his wife, who died in 1379, had bought a tomb. Was payment by the laity general, or at least an offering?[142]

Nobility were buried in the church and cloisters of Lucelle (Lützel, F) including eleven members of

---

[140] *NPS, passim; NBR,* p. 108; *NKN,* p. 155.
[141] *NC, passim.*
[142] *NPS, passim; NBR,* p. 108; *NSS,* p. 152.

the Hasenburg family. Clerics buried in a cloister included in 1484 Jerome, a monk but also suffragan bishop of Bamberg, interred at Langheim 'near the raised altar'. At Tennenbach (G) were interred, amongst others, the lords of Gysenberg, Stein, Landsberg and Bernhausen, the last two at least in the cloister. As for the outdoor cemetery, little appears in the necrologies, save that Conrad, dean of Munich, procured 'the lamp of the dead' for the cemetery at Fürstenfeld (G).[143]

For some monks in later centuries political and religious upheavals meant that they would not be interred in their own abbey church, for that may have been secularised or even lie in ruins. So it was that in 1581 Baldwin Valle, a monk of Baudeloo, died in Cologne. In 1784 Gregory Mambour, jubilarian and former bursar of Villers, was its first monk to be buried in its external cemetery. Salem witnessed the sad case of Zacharias Hanflig, a *conversus* and woollen worker, 'who after the secularisation of the monastery became mentally ill, and was taken to his native Pforzheim, where in 1807 he died and was buried'.[144]

SEPULCHRAL MONUMENTS

Several necrologies refer to the nature of grave monuments and tombstones, and their epitaphs.[145] That of

---
[143] *NLC*, pp. 42–4; *NLH*, p. 291; *NT*, p. 341; *NFN*, p. 98.
[144] *NB* f. 21v; *NV*, p. 79; *NSL*, p. 135.
[145] For those at Ebrach, see *Brevia Notitia Monasterii Ebracensis*,

Sepulchral Monuments

Ebrach (G) tells of Blessed Adam as being the first abbot, 'taking the habit whilst St Bernard lived', and abbot there for thirty-four years, from 1126 to 1161. The necrology relates that 'by the ancient fathers' he was accorded the epitaph 'Here lies the virtuous Adam in a great tomb, of Ebrach the first, his was a fine reward'.[146] Martin Krabb, monk of Heiligenkreuz (A) and described as a 'musician of fame', had a five-line epitaph which included the phrase 'buried in the tomb of the cantors'. At Pairis (F) the Latin inscription on the tomb of Anne de Cimeterio ran: 'Anna, may God always give you the food of the angels'. Other tombs might be simpler, such as that of Nicholas Teyn (*ob.* 1435) at Lilienfeld (A), 'a marble stone, with a gold cross'.[147]

At Boulancourt (F), Bishop Henry of Troyes, who gave the site to St Bernard in 1152, was buried on the gospel side of the sanctuary 'in a tomb raised in the manner of an altar'; and his successor, Bishop Matthew, was interred in the same tomb. In 1236 the count and countess of Urach were buried in the cemetery at Tennenbach (G) 'under a great sepulchral stone'. At Lucelle (Lützel, F) the tomb of Bishop Caspar of Basle (*ob.* 1502) bore the figure of a bishop with his heraldry, whilst the grave there by the altar of Ss Peter and Paul of a baron of Morpurgo was an arched monument.[148]

Rome, 1739, pp. 15–22.
[146] *NEBR*, p. 130; .
[147] *NLH*, pp 293–4; *NPS*, p. 75; *NLD*, p. 372.
[148] *NBL*, pp. 329–30 (*NBL*, p. 329: in 1283, Gauthier, lord of

Baldwin, dean of Frisia (*ob.* 1366), bequeathed forty-two groats to the nuns of St Servaas, Utrecht, of which the sacristan was to receive two groats, 'for her labour each year in cleaning and washing from dirt and dust the tomb of the lord bishop at his anniversary, and for sprinkling straw around the tomb and flowers with branches of green foliage', but the bishop is not named.[149]

BUILDING WORK

A necrology might note building work, either of new edifices or of necessary renovations. Much of this relates to the seventeenth and eighteenth centuries, as related later. It was something that the sisters of Marche-les-Dames (B) appreciated in their obituary, when they remembered on 3 December each year 'Francis of Senzeille, monk of Jardinet (B), our procurator and bursar for nineteen years, who did much good for the house, especially for the buildings, whether outside or inside of our bounds; taking care of and repairing the stable of the horses; the chamber of the guests above the postern gate; and the chamber of the abbess'. Soleilmont (B) received a grant around 1700 'for the chambers of the dorter'. Did this mean new cubicles for its nuns, rather than sleeping in common?[150]

 Villemalu, was buried 'on the side of the epistle'); *NT*, p. 338; *NLC*, pp. 40–1, 44.
[149] *NSS*, pp. 118–19.
[150] *NMD*, p. 192; *NSO*, p. 392.

THE GATE HOUSE AND THE POOR

The gate house was the point of entry into the monastic precinct, and the domain of the porter.[151] Here travellers dismounted, and here the poor received alms, especially on Maundy Thursday, that great day of charity. Here some of the business of the monastery might be transacted, and here manorial courts might be held—so we read at Lilienfeld (A) of Gregory Wishofa, 'once judge at the gate', and of Elizabeth Pheslin, 'wife of the judge at the gate'. Monastic judges are noted at Stams: Hanns Walther and Simon Fras, 'once our faithful judge', and at Raitenhaslach (G) 'Hanns Schneizer, judge of this monastery'.[152]

Monastic porters would normally be monks or *conversi*, but as the centuries progressed laymen might fulfil the role. There might also then be female assistants at the gate, as at Neuencamp (G): 'Lutghard, handmaid at the gate, who gave the church forty marks', and other assistants, such as Thomas 'our old bath-keeper at the gate' at Lilienfeld. Lay porters generally served the nunneries, such as Henry Jadinet at Marche-les-Dames (B), who left the convent thirteen florins, and at Port-Royal (F), 'Louis, our porter (*ob.* 1702), who had been a gardener on the granges'.

---

[151] Cf. David H. Williams, *The Cistercians in the Early Middle Ages*, 1992, pp. 200–4.
[152] *NLD*, p. 409; *NL*, p. 58; *NST*, pp. 51, 56; *NR*, p. 269.

The Latin word *caupo* may imply inn-keepers by the gate, as noted at Rein (A) and Wilhering (A).[153]

Religious who served as porters included at Salem (A) a monk, Balthasar Sonntag (*ob*. 1607), and a *conversus*, Martin Koler (*ob*. 1671). At Jędrzejów (P) a monk porter was Laurence (*ob*. 1434); at Kamieniec (P), Jacob (*ob*. 1572), and at St-Bernard-sur-l'Escaut (B), John de Monbe (*ob*. 1570), jubilarian.[154] Lay porters included Laurence Speckhart at Bronnbach, 'our porter and for forty years a servant'; Arnold Haaz (*ob*. 1693) at Boneffe, 'porter and benefactor of this house', whilst at Fürstenzell, Peter Schenperger had been its 'very faithful porter'.[155]

One of the duties of a porter was to distribute alms to the poor waiting outside the abbey gate. Livin de Smit (*ob*. 1614), monk of Bornem, was its porter and almoner. The necrology of Lilienfeld states that: 'We give on the Thursday after Easter in alms at the gate house three hundred loaves and two tuns of wine' (surely a mistranscription for: on the Thursday *before* Easter, for Maundy Thursday was the chief day of charity). A donor of Lilienfeld insisted that 'charity was to be given at the gate, as it was in the days of the founder, Duke Leopold',[156] for benevolence had been a feature of the Order from its beginnings.

---

[153] NN, p. 514; NLD, p. 420; NMD, p. 173; NPRL2, p. 627; NRE, pp. 342, 351; NW, pp. 87, 133.
[154] NSL, pp. 196, 75; NJD, p. 773; NKM, image 14; NBM, p. 19.
[155] NBR, p. 132; NBN, p. 290; NF, p. 126.
[156] NBM, p. 1; NL, p. 71; NLD, pp. 384, 406.

The Gate House and the Poor

Fürstenfeld (G) received a sack of rye 'for distributing bread to the poor'. Neuencamp received a grant 'for ever of forty marks of Lübeck money' in two instalments—at Easter and Michaelmas—'for the necessities of the poor at the gate', as well as eight shillings to be give yearly on 1 July 'for the well-being of the poor at the gate'. Engelszell (A) received a substantial sum of money from a donor for keeping his *obit* on 2 April each year, but also on that day 'for the adequate refreshment of three poor people'.[157]

The necrology of Pairis (F) informs us that from each 18 September, the brethren kept a solemn *Tricensium*, when each day for thirty days three portions were to be given to the poor. The nuns of Marche-les-Dames (B) were left five measures of spelter (an old kind of wheat eaten as a health food)[158] for distribution to the poor. These are but a few examples, and one can only imagine the struggle the weaker poor may have had to avail themselves of these benefits.[159]

Several obituaries make mention of 'the hospital of the poor' or 'secular infirmary', where poor and infirm people might reside on a permanent basis in a purposely constructed building, usually located close to the gate house, so as not to unduly disturb life within the cloister. This lay hospital at Heiligenkreuz (A) was said in 1232 to be 'sumptuously con-

---

[157] *NFN*, p. 102; *NN*, pp. 512, 517; *NE*, p. 243.
[158] *Concise Oxford English Dictionary*, 2011, p. 1388.
[159] *NPS*, p. 85; *NMD*, p. 169, respectively.

structed' (i.e. well built).[160] The hospital at Aldersbach (G) 'for the care and well-being of the poor and the sick' was built and endowed by a canon of Passau; that at Lilienfeld (G) by Heinrich Chastner, 'who built a house at the gate for a hospital, where food and drink are supplied by the cellarer', and that at Wilhering (A) by Wernhard of Schaurnberch.[161]

The necrology of Selingenthal nunnery (G) speaks of Hermann Hofsteter (*ob.* 1508), 'chaplain in the hospital, and our sincere supporter', and of H. Datz, 'master of the hospital', and of Martin Mair, a doctor, presumably on call. The lay hospital at Rein (A) had its own chapel dedicated to St Benedict. For their hospitals, Vyšší Brod (C) received a financial grant from Agnes of Walesee (*ob.* 1402), and Aldersbach gained income from possessions in Rudmansfeld.[162] The hospital at Fürstenzell (G) was founded by Hainrich of Radekeh, whilst its necrology tells us: 'Cristan Weterberg gave us money for the community, and for the thirty poor people in our hospital'.[163]

Many Cistercian monasteries also had a hospice for weary travellers, and both Popes Honorius III (1220)[164] and Gregory IX (1232),[165] noting their 'hospitality given to wayfarers and the poor', permitted them

---

[160] J. N. Weis, *Urkunden des Cistercienser-Stiftes Heiligenkreuz* 1, pp. 78–9.
[161] *NA*, p.183; *NW*, p. 169.
[162] *NSA*, pp. 486, 507; *NRE*, p. 349; *NHN*, pp. 387–8; *NA*, p. 23.
[163] *NF*, pp. 119, 123.
[164] G. Rupfer, ed., *Die Urkunden des Klosters Leubus*, Breslau, 1821, pp. 77–8.
[165] Weis, *Urkunden* 1, pp. 59–60 (XLVII).

The Gate House and the Poor

to increase their possessions so as to gain income to sustain this ministry. For Soleilmont (B) John Yernaux 'gave much for the repair of the chapel of St Nicholas, and the new works at the guest quarters'.[166]

Their necrologies tell of a *conversus* master of the hospice at Salem (A), of Gotfrid being a servant at the hospice of Lilienfeld, and of Christina at Wettingen (Sw), a lay lady and mistress of the hospice. Two of the guest-masters of Raitenhaslach (G) are named, but not dated: John Franck (also its baker) and George Chüestainer. At Bebenhausen (G), in 1271, Hainrich was the guest-master, and Eberhard the 'second guest-master'; they were both monks.[167]

A significant architectural feature was the gate-house chapel, where local people as well as residents might hear Mass. Such chapels are on record at Aldersbach (G; where Conrad of Gumphrecting 'provided for two Masses'); Engelszell (A; built by Otto de Zalking); Fürstenzell (G; dedicated to St Margaret); and Lilienfeld (A; dedicated to the Holy Trinity).[168] At Pairis (F), a new gate-house chapel was consecrated in 1469, 'in honour of the Holy Trinity, the Blessed Virgin Mary, and Ss Philip and Matthew, apostles'. For Wilhering (A) Otto Hoffpeck (*ob.* 1406) provided for 'Mass at the gate'.[169]

---

[166] *NSO*, p. 395.
[167] *NSL*, p. 221; *NLD*, p. 379; *NWT*, p. 591, *NR*, pp. 269, 273; *NBE*, p. 264.
[168] *NA*, p. 20; *NE*, p. 242; *NF*, p. 110; *NLD*, p. 423.
[169] *NPS*, p. 71; *NWL*, p. 450.

At Stams (A) a chapel of St John stood outside the gate, requiems were said there, and at one time it was served by a secular priest, John Taigscher. The chapel at the gate of Tennenbach (G) 'was built [in 1310] by the lords Brumen of Hornberg in honour of Ss Benedict, Peter and William, bishops in the Cistercian Order, and of Saint Scholastica, and of all confessors', but, its necrology tells us, it was destroyed in the *rusticorum seditio*, perhaps the uprising of the peasantry in 1525.[170] The chapel, restored, exists to-day.[171]

CISTERCIAN BISHOPS

Necrologies, from the later medieval times onwards, tell of several Cistercian abbots, particularly in Poland, who were raised to episcopal office, though sometimes to a titular see *in partibus infidelium*. Abbot Nicholas Reuse of Oliwa (1469–74) was consecrated to the titular see of Gallipoli. A monk of Sulejów, Nicholas Mscziwy (*ob.* 1526), and John Madaleński, former abbot of Ląd (*ob.* 1644), acted as suffragan bishops of Poland's ecclesiastical capital, Gniezno, whilst Laurence Gębicki (*ob.* 1624), also a Cistercian, became archbishop of that see.[172]

Abbots *in commendam* included Bishop Laurence Goslicki (*ob.* 1607) of Poznan, 'the first abbot admin-

---

[170] *NST*, p. 55; *NT*, pp. 339–40.
[171] B. Peugniez, *Le Guide routier de l'Europe cistercienne*, Strasbourg, 2012, pp. 521–2.
[172] *NOL*, p. 509; *NJD*, p. 775; *NLA*, p. 474.

istrator' at Mogiła, and Augustine Wessel (*ob.* 1735), bishop of Kamieniec, noted as being the 'regular abbot' of Jędrzejów. Anthony Bartholomew Nałęcz Raczyński (*ob.* ?1800), for thirty years abbot of Ląd, was for twelve years titular bishop of 'Hetalonensis'.[173] Three former abbots of Pelplin held the see of Chełmno: Francis Czapski (*ob.* 1733), Valentine Czapski (*ob.* 1751) and Adalbert Leski (*ob.* 1758). Abbot Simon Ranst of Valdieu (B) was elected bishop of nearby Roermond in 1658. Abbot John Ladislas Pyrker (*ob.* 1847) of Lilienfeld became patriarch of Venice and then archbishop of Eger.[174]

ABBOTS AND ABBESSES/PRIORESSES

A lengthy abbacy could be helpful, as that of Nicholas Anthony Lukomski (*ob.* 1750), abbot of Ląd (P) for fifty-three years; he was noted as 'the father of the poor, the guardian of orphans'. Nicholas Odrowąsz was abbot of Jędrzejów (P; *ob.* 1496) for fifty years, whilst at Lilienfeld (A), Abbot Matthew III (*ob.* 1695) was listed as 'a meritorious abbot who ruled happily for forty-five years', as did Joseph John Szołdrski (*ob.* 1797) at Przemet (P).[175]

Several abbots served for thirty years or more, such as Stephen Zusatz (*ob.* 1398), abbot of Lilienfeld

---

[173] *NML*, p. 813; *NJD*, pp. 776; *NLA*, p. 479–80.
[174] *NLA*, pp. 485, 495; *NC*, p. 106; *NKN*, p. 26; *NNC*, n.p.
[175] *NLA*, p. 485; *NJD*, p. 778; *NL*, p. 44.

(A) for thirty-eight years, and Abbot Ambrose Balbus (*ob* 1794), who ruled Bronnbach (G) for thirty-one years, then retired, dying eleven years later at the age of ninety-four. In modern times both branches of the Order have elected abbots-general, such as Leopold Watzkarsch (*ob*. 1901), who was for forty-four years abbot of Vyšší Brod (C), and at the age of eighty-two became abbot-general of the Order of Cîteaux, whilst Abbot Benedict Littwerig (*ob*. 1726) had been its vicar-general.[176]

As for the nunneries, at Marche-les-Dames (B) and elsewhere, there was a process of renewal in the mid-fifteenth century, commonly called 'the reform'. Its necrology suggests that its first prioress following the reform, Mary Leblanc, ruled for forty years, but modern listing of the prioresses suggests that this cannot be the case. If she was Marie III of Herstel, then her term of office from 1460 to 1486 lasted but twenty-six years. The necrology is correct in relating that the ninth prioress after the reform held office for thirty-two years; in fact she ruled from 1602 to 1635.[177]

The obituary of Port-Royal des Champs (F) lists forty-one abbesses between 1227 and 1706. It too knew reform under a titular abbess, Mother Marie Angelique, who ruled for twenty-seven years, dying in 1661; in 1669 a miraculous healing was attributed to her intercession. Mother Marie-Genevieve (*ob*. 1646) is recorded as being its 'first abbess by

---

[176] *NLD*, p. 369; *NBR*, p. 113; *NNC*, n.p.
[177] *NMD*, p. 155.

election'. Their necrologies tell of their character. Jehanne de la Fin (*ob.* 1522), abbess for forty-five years, strongly defended the rights of the church at the time of Lutheranism, 'and recovered the goods and lands which had been plundered and lost during the years of war'. Abbess Agnes de Ligni (*ob.* 1675) knew imprisonment during troubled times.[178]

When Abbess Jacqueline Colnetz (*ob.* 1639) of Soleilmont passed away aged eighty-eight, having been professed for seventy years, it was noted that she had 'governed the house for thirty-six years in extreme peace and tranquillity'. The *obit* of Ludovica Zarebianka (*ob.* 1794), prioress of Owińska for twenty-two years, tells that she was 'full of days and of merit, fulfilling her office with all charity and glorious affability'. The prioress of the same house, Melchiora Gurowska, died in 1802, aged seventy-nine after being prioress for thirty-three years and three months. She, too, was 'full of days and merit', and praised for the example she set.[179]

The necrology of Fürstenfeld (G) lists its abbots from Volkmar, the fifth abbot (*ob.* 1314, after an abbacy of thirty years), down to Leonard, the eighteenth abbot (*ob.* 1496). The average length of an abbacy there was seventeen years, and no recorded abbot served for fewer than ten years. The necrology of Altenberg (G) lists twenty-two abbots, ranging from

---

[178] *NPRL*, pp. lxix, 302–11; *NPRL2*, p. 495; *NPR*, pp. 644–5; *NPRL2*, p. 613.
[179] *NSO*, p. 394; *NKN*, pp. 111, 130.

Gottfrid (*ob.* 1168) the first abbot, down to Andrew (*ob.* 1519), the first mitred abbot of the house. Four abbesses of Baindt (G) can be traced as resigning their position, such as Anne Tannerin, who died in 1722 aged eighty, having ruled for thirty-four years before her retirement.[180]

An abbacy was normally held for life, but resignations were not unknown. Abbot Meinward of Tennenbach (G; *ob.* 1317) abdicated, but shortly afterwards died whilst on a journey. Abbot Colomann II of Heiligenkreuz (A) resigned in 1392. Abbot Martin of Szent Gotthard (H; *ob.* 1478) resigned 'out of humility'. Abbot Gilbert of Baudeloo (B) died in 1326 on his way home from attending General Chapter, and was buried at Foigny abbey.[181]

On occasion a monastery might feel the need to elect an abbot from another house. In Poland Ląd provided superiors, amongst others, to Jędrzejów (Abbot Stephen, *ob.* 1681), Koprzynica (Abbot Francis, *ob.* 1737) and Obra (Abbot Stanislas, *ob.* 1690, and Abbot William, *ob.* 1744). Mogiła gave abbots to Bledzew (Abbot Praemislaus, *ob.* 1704); Imielnica (Abbot Gregory, not dated), and to Szczyrzycz (Abbot Stanislas, *ob.* 1538).[182] From 1538, by Polish law, only a Pole could hold the abbacy of a monastery, and so John Wysocki (*ob.* 1560) became the first Polish abbot of Ląd. At Villers (B), Laurence Dieu had

---

[180] *NFN, passim; NAL*, pp. 339–44; *NBT*, pp. 232, 239, 242.
[181] *NT*, p. 339; *NHG, passim; NNC*, n.p; *NB*, f. 42r.
[182] *NJD*, p. 782; *NLA*, pp. 477, 480, 483.

been nominated as abbot in 1676, 'but falling from his seat he broke an arm and his life and nomination came to an end'.[183]

Necrologies might laud their former abbots. For Lucelle (Lützel, F), we learn how its twenty-sixth abbot, Conrad Holzacker, spoke at the Council of Constance (around 1410), and for Zwettl (A), we read of Abbot Wolfgang Oertl (*ob.* 1508), who 'did much good for the monastery'; for Fürstenzell (G) we hear of Abbot Achaius (*ob.* 1457), 'who erected buildings, and took us out of debt'; and for Mogiła of Abbot Theodore (*ob.* 1709), who 'after a hundred years and more, happily delivered Mogiła from the hands of commendatories'. At Villers, Idesbald Wilmaert, its fifty-second abbot, was noted as 'a pious and holy man'. Abbot for only four years (1667–71), the record tells that when in later years new paving was laid in the church, 'his body and cowl were found intact and incorrupt'. In 1553, at Aulps, John Trolliet, 'the humble abbot of this monastery', died from hydropsy.[184]

Abbots had their own quarters and household. The necrologies tell us of Abbot John Zanker, the twenty-fourth abbot of Aldersbach (G, *ob.* 1552), 'who made the special building of the abbot', and at Wilhering (A) we learn of Stephen de Wegschayd (*ob.* 1509), chaplain of the abbot, and of Otto Swarcz-

---

[183] *NLA*, p. 474; *NV*, p. 61.
[184] *NLC*, p. 225; *NZ*, p. 569; *NF*, p. 108; *NML*, p. 809; *NV*, p. 61; *NAP*, p. 128.

pekch, his servant; at Salem (A) of the abbot's secretary; at Roermond of Thomas Heeler, chaplain of its abbess; at Ląd of the abbot's scribe; at Bebenhausen of Albert, monk, the abbot's notary, and at Pelplin (P), of the abbot's hunter.[185] Interestingly, the necrology of Aldersbach notes the *obit* of Dietmar, 'master of the hunters at Byburg'. Bartholomew Zimmermann was in 1577 the abbot's kitchen-master at Oliwa (P).[186]

Prized by some abbots was the right to wear the mitre and other pontifical accessories. It was a privilege accorded to Abbot Andrew of Fürstenfeld, who spoke at the Council of Basle in 1431. A few necrologies tell us the date of death of the first abbot of a house to receive this honour: in 1445 (death of Abbot Rudolph of Wettingen, Sw); in 1448 (death of Abbot John of Aldersbach); in 1488 (death of Abbot Godfrey of Orval, B), in 1519 (death of Abbot Andrew of Altenburg, G), in 1551 (death of Jerome Feigl of Heilgenkreuz (A); and in 1552 (death of Abbot Nicholas of Rudy, P).[187]

The necrology of Ebrach (G) suggests that the eleventh abbot of Langheim (G), John Nobilis (*ob*. 1379), had received this privilege from Pope Sixtus IV, but he reigned from 1471 to 1484 when John Schad was the abbot. A mistake here somewhere!

---

[185] *NA*, p. 15; *NW*, pp. 57, 149; *NSL*, p. 107; *NRM*, p. 20; *NLA*, p. 499; *NBE*, p. 265; *NPL*, p. 87.
[186] *NA*, p. 8; *NOL1*, p. 139.
[187] *NFN*, p. 97; *NHN*, p. 388; *NWT*, p. 593; *NA*, p.11; *NO*, p. 231; *NAL*, p. 344; *NNC*, n.p; *NJD*, p. 788.

Priors

Lilienfeld, at an unknown date, received the gift of a mitre.[188]

PRIORS

The second-in-command was the prior. At Bronnbach (G), Caspar Geys (*ob.* 1640) was 'a most vigilant prior for thirty years'. By 1660, when he died, Melchior was the 'emeritus prior' of Kamieniec (P), whilst Matthias (*ob.* 1590), prior of Pelplin (P), died 'at the nineteenth hour on the 26 August'.[189] We learn from the obituary of Villers (B) of Theodore Beeckman (*ob.* 1600), 'a distinguished and exemplary prior', and of John Finet (*ob.* 1609), 'an exemplary and dedicated prior'. Martin Lejuin (*ob.* 1782) was 'a rigid and austere prior' there, whilst Albert Wesy (*ob.* 1786) served 'by word and example'. Diepold, prior of Schönau in 1184, became abbot of Bebenhausen in 1190, later returning as abbot of Schönau itself.[190]

Dying in 1468, Ulric Heghain, prior of Salem (A), had been a monk for forty years, and previously had been cantor, then sub-prior. Of Alexander Windisch (*ob.* 1706), prior of Neuberg (A) for thirty-one years, its necrology notes that he had been 'for many years a diligent labourer in the vineyard of the Lord'. Next

---

[188] *NEBR*, p. 195; *NLD*, p. 370.
[189] *NBR*, p. 100; *NKM*, image 17; *NPL*, p. 68. Again we have the names of the Wise Men, and also one Caspar (*ob.* 1467) was prior of Altenberg: *NAL*, p. 345
[190] *NV*, pp. 52, 54, 81; *NSC*, p. 107.

in line of authority was the sub-prior, such as Martin de Bus (*ob.* 1647), who occupied this position at Cambron (B), and was recorded as being 'a man of the greatest piety, and of wonderful virtue and abstinence'.[191]

THE MONKS

Necrologies can give some idea of the numerical strength of a community. At Bronnbach (G), of the 177 religious professed between 1640 and 1801, twenty-five were born in Würzburg, where the abbey had a major property. Of the period between 1629 and 1820 the age of death of ninety of its religious averaged sixty-five years, suggesting a fairly healthy community. Of the thirty monks noted in the brief necrology of St Urban (Sw), six were natives of Lucerne, and five were born at Solothurn. The 'book of the dead' of Koronowo notes some of the causes of death in the Polish houses, such as apoplexy, consumption, hydropsy, paralysis, phthisis (tuberculosis or the like), and 'morbid rheumatism'. For the eighteenth century it records the deaths of 371 religious in the Polish abbeys, their average age at death being just over fifty-six years. One had attained his ninetieth birthday, eleven were octogenarians, and sixteen died before their thirtieth birthday.[192]

[191] *NSL*, p. 4; *NNB*, p. 38; *NC*, p. 104.
[192] *NBR, passim*; *NSU, passim*; *NKN, passim*.

The Monks

The partial necrology of Aulps is unusual in that it lists the dates of entry into its novitiate of its religious, and names over fifty who did so between 1546 (when Francis de Ravorée, of one of the ancient families of Chablais, entered) and 1721. It also details the length of their formation. Stephen Tavernier, who became a novice in 1635, was ordained priest six years later in 1641. Claude Châtenoux, a native of Annecy, 'forsook the world' on New Year's Eve, 1643, took solemn vows on Maundy Thursday in 1650, and celebrated his first Mass at Michaelmas (29 September) in 1651. Between 1720 and 1721 four of its religious entered the novitiate at 'the arch-abbey of Clairvaux', its monks being dispersed.[193]

At Ebrach (G) between 1714 and 1779 sixty-six monks were professed, and nine *conversi*. During the abbacy of Ludovic (1686–1704) fourteen priest-monks were ordained, and four *conversi* professed. Of the monks in the house at this time, two died from dysentery; one was noted as 'fugitive'; another also left and married. Two retained their own name on profession, but later John Baptist Kraft, professed in 1791, assumed the name of Theodore. At Villers between 1574 and 1729, 380 monks were listed. Of those whose birth-place was noted, fifty-two monks were natives of Brussels, twenty-two of Namur, twelve of Louvain, and eleven of Wavre. A note of

---

[193] *NAP, passim*, especially pp. 127, 135, 137, 141: in 1711, Matthew Farrat, a novice of Aulps from 1684, celebrated his first Mass at Clairvaux.

the monks of Waverley (E), between 1312 and 1325, shows that they came from localities not too far distant, such as Salisbury and Winchester.[194] A small minority of monks died before they could be professed, such as John Radzimieński (*ob.* 1609) and Peter Kulick (*ob.* 1613) at Jędrzejów (P). Early novices at St-Bernard-sur-l'Escaut (B) included a knight, Arnold of Haelbeke (*ob.* 1310). Solemn profession was a point of no return, and a servant of the abbot of Wettingen (Sw), John Voght (date not known), gave the community ten florins, 'from which we obtained thirty-two bowls of pure pewter in his memory, so that the rest of all the novices, making their profession, ought each to be given two bowls of excellent quality'. Before profession novices made their wills, such as Albert Seewaldt in 1741 at Oliwa (P), who bequeathed half of his estate for the sick of the abbey, and Florian Bach in 1743 who favoured his sister. Occasionally, a master of novices is noted, such as John Eysele at Fürstenzell (G).[195]

In the course of their monastic life monks might occupy several positions within their communities. At Bronnbach Eugene Burns (*ob.* 1739) had been cantor, granarian, bursar and then prior. At Salem Ulrich Hegain (*ob.* 1468), a monk there for forty years, had risen from cantor to sub-prior, and then to prior, whilst Guntram (*ob.* 1769), had fulfilled the roles of

---

[194] *NEBR*, pp. 262–3, 307; *NV, passim*; *NWV*, p. 116.
[195] *NJD*, pp. 780, 791; *NBM*, p. 35; *NWT*, pp. 594–5; *NOL3*, pp. 21, 23; *NF*, p. 116.

'kitchener, granarian, novice master, bursar, prior, and senior confessor of all nuns and convents'. His must have been a full life. A few monks transferred from one abbey to another, as did Paul Wilkowski (*ob.* 1598), professed at Mogiła, but dying as a monk of Jędrzejów (P); or even to another Order, as did John Mengaert of St-Bernard-sur-l'Escaut (B), who joined the Carthusians, but was still remembered in its obituary.[196]

JUBILARIANS

Monastic obituaries could proudly record the names of deceased jubilarians, monks professed for fifty years or more. Their longevity means that they will also have held various roles, as at Ebrach (G), where Adam Adelman (*ob.* 1823) had been, amongst other positions, keeper at the gate, sub-prior, master of the novices and *conversi*, later cellarer, and finally prior. Occasionally, they receive high praise, as did Mark Voelger (*ob.* 1796), monk of Salem (A), noted as being 'ardent in the love of God', whilst at Tennenbach it was reported of Blessed Hugh (*ob.* 1264), a monk for fifty-five years, that he had entered the monastery in 1209, and then 'lived in and lit up this place for fifty-five years'. His feast-day was 27 December. When he died in 1713, Stanislaus Szmyt, monk of Koronowo (P), was a centenarian. Its necrology

---

[196] *NBR*, 97; *NSL*, p. 74; *NLA*, p. 487; *NBM*, p. 42 (undated).

tells us that a nun of Soleilmont (B), Marie Piettre (*ob.* 1776), a jubilarian, had been its bursar for forty-six years. When she died in 1715, Maria Agatha Wehin was aged seventy-five, and had been a nun of Baindt (G) for fifty-eight years.[197]

CELLARERS

A major office was that of the cellarer, sometimes called 'the keeper' or *custos*. Many abbeys had a major cellarer, such as John of Uffolz (*ob.* 1341) at Pairis (F), and a sub-cellarer, such as Nicholas Nulaet (*ob.* 1382) at St-Bernard-sur-l'Escaut (B), or a 'minor cellarer', such as Constantine Reinhold (*ob.* 1799) at Hauterive (Sw), or 'under-cellarer', such as Walther (*ob.* 1276), so termed at Schönau (G). At Pilis (Hg), John, who died in 1299, was referred to as being 'claviger [keeper of the keys] and cellarer'. The names of several of the cellarers of Oliwa (P) are on record, such as Elger in 1277, John Camp in 1379 and John Scriptoris in 1435.[198]

The sub-cellarer of Lilienfeld (A) had a specific duty of caring for the wine, whilst at Salem there was a specified wine-cellarer, Leonard Bino (*ob.* 1687). Cellarers and bursars might be praised for their devotion to duty, such as John Kamerstetten, 'for

---

[197] *NEBR*, p. 299; *NSL*, p. 76; *NT*, p. 341; *NKN*, p. 13; *NSO*, p. 433; *NBT*, p. 233.
[198] *NPS*, p. 69; *NBM*, p. 58; *NHR*, p.108; *NSC*, p. 108; *NHG*, *passim*; *NOL1*, pp. 134–5.

Cellarers

thirty-three years a very devoted *custos'* at Fürstenzell (G), and at Kamieniec (P) John Pradelin (*ob.* 1633) 'faithful steward or bursar'. John Künlin fulfilled the role of bursar at Bebenausen (B) from 1484 to 1508.[199]

Cellarers, and in later days bursars, assisted by their monastic scribes, will have kept a careful record of all transactions pertaining to their monastery. At Fürstenzell it was Abbot Jacob (*ob.* 1397) himself who 'prepared the record of the sums and other goods given to this church'. At Tennenbach (G) it was John Meyer, monk and an 'industrious and diligent scribe' who, around the year 1341, compiled diligently 'an old *urbarium*' (i.e. a rent roll, perhaps with details of stock, and of an owner's rights over his men). John Puz (*ob.* 1579), the chamberlain of Aldersbach (G), gave the abbey, in return for the keeping of his wife's *obit*, twenty-four live sheep in perpetuity, 'as is shown by letters in writing'.[200]

A scribe, Sweigkerus, gave Fürstenzell (G) a rent of twelve florins, 'as shown by a deed in the bursary', while an annual rent of twenty florins, granted to it arising out of property at Entaw, was proved 'by letters made in 1468'. Denis Salmon, mayor of Namur, gave ten florins of rent to the nuns of Soleilmont (B) in return for his annual *obit*, 'as appears from his will of 6 February 1678'. Dame Antoinette of Vitry

---

[199] *NLD*, p.388; *NSL*, p. 130; *NF*, p. 125; *NKM*, image 37; *NBE*, p. 281.
[200] *NF*, p. 125; *NT*, p. 340; *NA*, p. 22.

demanded of Boulancourt (F), by her will of 1552, that 'her name be inscribed in the obituary'.[201]

Other evidence will have long been lost or unrecorded. As for scribes, Simon Moraski (*ob.* 1629), a layman but scribe for Pelplin (P), bequeathed 400 florins to that monastery. When the site of Tennenbach (G) was bought 'by the first abbot of Frienisberg and twelve monks', the transaction was mediated by 'the illustrious prince, Hermann, margrave of Hachberg, who confirmed the pact with his seal'.[202]

SCHOLARSHIP

Whilst most necrology entries regarding scholarship relate to early modern times, by the later Middle Ages a university degree was seen as a prerequisite to obtaining an abbacy. More than that, by this time some monastic houses were providing what would today be termed 'secondary education'. When she died in 1383, Beatrice of Sulen was a 'scholar' at St Servaas abbey in Utrecht, whilst Elisabeth of Oetrun, who died there in 1432, was referred to as 'nun and scholar of this place'. The nuns of Lilienthal may have employed a school-master named Berenger.[203]

At Marche-les-Dames (B) Catherine of Lovanio on dying was noted as 'scholar here, thirteen years

---

[201] *NF*, pp. 116, 124; *NSO*, p. 397; *NBL*, p. 329.
[202] *NPL*, p. 104; *NWT*, p. 590; *NT*, p. 338.
[203] *NSS*, pp. 152, 106; *NTK*, p. 532.

Scholarship

old'. The necrology of Billigheim (G) lists Irmentrude and Alheid (later a nun) as deceased scholars of the house. When plague struck Seligenthal (G) in 1495, eight girl scholars died. Two undated references, both seemingly to laity, tell of the *obit* of Dietmar de Lincza, scholar at Wilhering (A), and of Henry Alieigena at Raitenhaslach (G): 'educated here, and now has the distinction of bachelor'.[204] In the nineteenth century a biographical list from St Urban (Sw) shows that it had a monastery school. Amongst its monk-teachers were Urban Winistorter (*ob.* 1850), who taught mathematics, and Leopold Nägell (*ob.* 1874), a monk proficient at the organ and the clavier. Malachias Hegi (*ob.* 1865) instructed the junior monks in mathematics, calligraphy and drawing.[205]

Louvain had a university of excellence, and both Orval and Villers maintained colleges there for the residence of monks seeking a degree, whilst in Poland Abbot Nicholas Lukomski of Ląd (*ob.* 1750) 'instituted provincial studies in the college of Mogiła'. At Orval college, with one of its monks as president, between the years 1734 and 1750 at least twelve of its monks graduated as bachelors of sacred theology. The college of Villers was rebuilt by Abbot Martin Staignier (sixtieth abbot, 1742–59), and its necrology notes that: 'It is now not the least of the many fine colleges of the university'. Many other Cistercians

---

[204] *NMD*, p. 173; *NBH*, pp. 59, 62; *NSA*, p. 512; *NW*, p. 66; *NR*, p. 278.
[205] *NSU*, pp. 329–30, 332.

will have studied at Louvain, such as George Margraff (*ob*. 1730) of Bronnbach, who gained a doctorate there. Schönau (G) had a college in Heidelberg, where a monk, Elbald (*ob*. 1467), had been provisor; Salem had a school of philosophy.[206] Caspar Renner (*ob*. 1487), monk of Salem, was a Bachelor of Letters of the University of Paris; Stephen Ermlich (*ob*. 1761), monk of Neuberg, studied humanities at Melk and philosophy in Vienna, before becoming successively succentor, cantor, novice master and professor in philosophy and theology at his monastery. Alas, a young monk of Bronnbach (G), William Moll (*ob*. 1614), still a deacon, died in Rome whilst a student at the German college there. Between 1580 and 1600 six monks of Oliwa (P), before they entered the novitiate, had studied under the Jesuits at Braunsberg, Prussia.[207]

The list of Cistercian scholars is endless, such as Abbot Henry V of Ebrach (G; 1447–55): 'A tall, handsome and peaceful man, learned, eloquent, a bacheor of theology, and accomplished in rhetoric'. Stephen, a monk of Neuencamp (G), was 'a doctor of sacred theology, and bachelor of sacred decrees, of laudable life, conversation and patience'. John Zenli (*ob*. 1353), the eleventh abbot of Tennenbach (G), was noted to be 'a very religious and learned man'. The twenty-second abbot of Du Val (F), John

---

[206] *NLA*, p.285; *NO, passim*; *NV*, pp. 74–5; *NBR*, p. 96; *NSC*, p. 109; *NBE*, p. 298.
[207] *NSL*, 74; *NNB*, pp. 40–1; *NBR*, p. 133; *NOL1*, pp. 139–40, 177, 179, 200–1.

Scholarship

of Montebirella (*ob.* 1440), was a doctor of theology. Abbot John III of Heiligenkreuz (A; *ob.* 1459), formerly a monk of Bronnbach and a doctor of theology, was a professor at Vienna University, and Abbot Vincent Gruner of Altzelle (*ob.* 1442) was once rector of Leipzig University. A monk of Cambron (B), Andrew Enobarbius (*ob.* 1538), was 'a man erudite in all science'.[208]

Back home in their monasteries Cistercian graduates were able to teach to the juniors a wide variety of subjects. At Salem (A) Melchior Mayr (*ob.* 1760) was 'moderator of the studies of the juniors'. Eberhard Eisele (*ob.* 1803) was 'erudite in mathematics and geometry', and Philip Fridl (*ob.* 1808), covered philosophy, mathematics, physics, astronomy, theology, church history and canon law', whilst Jerome Buchet (*ob.* 1818) was 'an instructor in studies of the Greek language'.[209]

At Neuberg (A), Ferdinand Hauzenberger (*ob.* 1795) was professor in philosophy and moral theology, and also cellarer. The obituary of Jędrzejów (P) tells both of its own scholars, such as Luke Ianocky (*ob.* 1624), bachelor of arts and philosophy, and also of a monk of Mogiła (P), Jacob (*ob.* 1421), a master of arts and a bachelor of sacred theology. At St Urban (Sw), Conrad Effinger, prior from 1839 to 1848, was professor in dogmatic and moral theology and

---

[208] *NEBR*, p. 202; *NN*, p. 514; *NT*, p. 341; *NVA*, p. 631; *NNC*, n.p; *NC*, p. 104.
[209] *NSL, passim.*

church history. A monk of Ląd (P), Urban Brunowski, taught at several places, and in 1805 died at Pelplin. Gabriel Heinrich taught philosophy and theology at Bledzew (P; *ob.* 1802) for twenty-two years.[210] Several monks expressed their knowledge in their writings. By 1679 Oliwa (P) had it own printing press with a monk, Augustine Hoffman, in charge. The several necrologies tell of Ambrose, a monk of Jędrzejów, 'who wrote much', and of Placid, monk of Ląd (P), 'who wrote ecclesiastical books'. Perthold (*ob.* 1324), a monk of Zwettl (A), 'wrote the books in our chapter-house'.[211] At Fürstenzell (G) Prior John Gundelsoder (*ob.* 1456) was 'the writer of many books', whilst at Tennenbach, a monk, Symon (*ob.* 1457), 'wrote the anniversary book of the monastery of Güntersthal'. A monk of Lilienfeld (A), Nicholas Pownveint (*ob.* 1490), 'whilst a guest at Hohenfurt [Vyšší Brod (C)], wrote there a psalter in membrane'. The obituary of Lucelle (Lützel, F) lists those monks who wrote praiseworthy works, such as its thirtieth abbot, Theobald Hylweg (1495–1532), who compiled the annals of the house, and a monk, Christopher Schaller (*ob.* 1642), who composed spiritual works, including one regarding 'the perfection of religion'.[212]

The obituary of Villers (B) tells of Paul Chifflet (*ob.* 1688), formerly a monk there, but later abbot of Mont-Sainte-Marie in Burgundy, as 'erudite and

---

[210] *NNB*, p. 43; *NJD*, pp. 782, 801; *NSU*, p. 328; *NKN*, pp. 137, 133, respectively.
[211] *NOL2*, p. 1; *NJD*, 803; *NLA*, p. 478; *NZ* p. 572
[212] *NF*, p. 110; *NT*, p. 340; *NL*, p. 141; *NLC*, pp. 227, 231.

author of praiseworthy works', noting that he was listed in the *Bibliotheca Auctorum Ordinis Cisterciensis*. George Neuberger (*ob.* 1717), monk of Ebrach, was listed as a notable author in history and philosophy, specialising in subjects such as predestination and reason, even when for a time 'detained in the monastery prison'. Nor were all the medieval *conversi* unlettered: Conrad Teufel (*ob.* 1339) of Ebrach (G) was noted for a celebrated apologetic work, *Diaboliorum Herbipolensium Patritiorum*.[213]

LIBRARIES AND BOOKS

Monastic obituaries give us a glimpse of the wealth of volumes which certain monasteries accumulated before their dissolution, necessitating, for example, the construction of a new library at Ebrach during the abbacy of Ludovic (1686–96), and the cataloguing of its books. Copying of works, and the preparation of new manuscripts, was the work of monastic scribes, such as the two monks at Jędrzejów (P), Bernard and Frederick, 'monks and scribes'. The nuns of Seligenthal (G) employed lay 'cloister scribes', such as Udalric Kirmir and Sigismund Milhofer, and also Michael Weilinger, 'our counter-writer'.[214]

---

[213] *NV*, p. 64; *NEBR*, p. 259; *NEBR*, p. 172.
[214] *NEBR*, p. 262; *NLD*, pp. 369, 371; *NSA*, pp. 493, 496, 511 ('gegenschreiber').

Care of manuscripts was the responsibility of monastic archivists, such as Berthold Wartha (*ob.* 1802), a monk at Salem (A), and Felix Ratt (*ob.* 1820), a *conversus* there. Somewhat earlier, John, a familiar, was the archivist of Kamieniec (P). One of the named librarians of Salem was a monk, Meinrad Rosenzweig (*ob.* 1780), whilst at Lucelle (Lützel, F) Bernard Buchinger was for fifteen years both archivist and librarian, compiling the obituaries both of Lucelle and Pairis (F). At Vyšší Brod (C), a monk, Benedict Holzbauer (*ob.* 1868), also fulfilled that dual role.[215]

The building up of a monastic library was greatly aided by generous gifts of books, not least those relating to the scriptures. Wettingen (Sw) profited from a donation of 'the whole Bible, and moreover ten volumes of the best books', as well as a gift of 'eight good books'; Engelszell (A) received two volumes of the Bible, and Pelplin (P) 'a good book, namely a lyric upon the Psalms', as well as three other books regarding Balaam, Abel, and Gregory secundus Ezekiel'.[216] Gerard of Verton gave Orval (B) not only commentaries on the Four Gospels, but also one hundred Paris pounds! Gregory Pyff of Neuenburg gave Wilhering (A), 'from friendship', three volumes, 'namely the Old and New Testaments, and the Book of Sentences, on paper'.[217]

---

[215] *NSL*, pp. 222, 133; *NKM*, image 10; *NSL*, p. 37; *NLC*, p. 221; *NNC*, n.p.
[216] *NWT*, p. 522; *NE*, p. 247; *NPL*, pp. 91, 94.
[217] *NO*, p. 224; *NW*, p. 89.

Kaisheim (G) received thirty volumes from a local rector; whilst Otto of Gnemhertel gave 'forty good volumes to Zwettl' (A); alas, he died in 1349 from the Black Death. Bronnbach received 'his small library' from Melchior Eigenbrod (*ob.* 1661), priest in Newbron, as well as three chasubles,[218] whilst John Sculteti (*ob.* 1523), archdeacon of Warmia, left Pelplin 'all his books', and a fellow canon gave that abbey a work entitled 'Observations on the Law', whilst a canon of Colberg donated 'A Summary of the Faith'. Baudeloo (B) was bequeathed two Flemish books by John Baptist Duellens.[219] There is frequent reference to the volumes donated as being 'good books'.

THE NUNS

Cistercian nunneries varied considerably in the numbers of their religious. The necrology of Marche-les-Dames (B) covers only the latter part of its history, but enumerates approximately 220 nuns, 120 *conversae*, four male *conversi*, sixteen male familiars and nine female familiars. The obituary of St Servaas in Utrecht gives the *obits* of twenty-two abbesses, some one hundred nuns, almost twenty 'sisters' (*conversae*), and four male *conversi*, the latter attached to convents for tasks physically difficult for the nuns. The appendices attached to the necrology of Seligenthal (Lands-

---

[218] *NKH*, p. 89; *NZ*, p. 71; *NBR*, p. 127.
[219] *NPL*, pp. 112–13; *NPL*, p. 92; *NPL*, p. 99, *NB*, f. 12.

hut; G) tell of the presence over its long history of 439 nuns and 62 female *conversae*, as well as 139 male *conversi*. The *obit* list of Sonnenfeld convent names thirty-three male *conversi* serving the house between 1273 and 1390, including a shoemaker, a baker, a brewer, procurators and waiters. Thirty-eight male *conversi* are on record as serving the nuns of Gnadenthal between 1253 and 1370.[220]

The record of Argenton (B) lists the dates of death of 267 abbesses and nuns, down to the closure of the abbey in 1796. Of these, seventy-five died in the two winter months of January and February. The listing also includes the *obits* of 119 *conversae*, ranging from 1420 onwards, as well as those of twenty familiars, male and female, mostly from the later centuries of the nunnery's history. When the abbey was suppressed in December 1796, the roll call was of sixteen nuns and eight *conversae*. The necrology of Feldbach (Sw) lists the names of a few abbesses and 155 nuns, but has no separate mention of *conversae*.[221]

The obituary of Port-Royal-des-Champs (F) tells of the clothing of novices at the young ages of seven and nine. One, Sister Elizabeth de Sainte Agnes le Feron, entered at the age of seven, took the white veil in 1652, pronounced her vows in 1654 (when about twenty-one), and died aged seventy-three in 1706. Certain of its nuns were highly thought of, such as

---

[220] *NMD, passim; NSS*, pp. 104–60; *NSA*, pp. 513–20; *NSN*, p. 332; *NGn*, p. 138.
[221] *NAR*, pp. 202–40; *NFD, passim*.

The Nuns

Matilda Mauni, 'sacred to God, a mirror of humility', and Anne de Sainte Monique (*ob*. 1657), who four years before her death had transferred from the Benedictine Order 'to live a more exact observance'. A nun might die young, as did Benedicta Cieńska of Ołobok (P), dying in 1800 aged but twenty, and professed for only four years.[222]

At Marche-les-Dames (B) Margaret Christian, once a Jewess, was professed at the age of sixteen. Daughters of the nobility were prominent in many nunneries, as at Gnadenthal (G), the *obit* list of which stressed the parentage and siblings of the sisters. One such was Mechtild (*ob*. 1266), daughter of Count Gottfried of Löwenstein; her own blood sister was the abbess of Cistercian Lichtenstern.[223]

The strict enclosure of the nuns meant that, in addition to resident male *conversi*, there was often a resident monk acting as provost and, in conjunction with the abbess, having oversight of the nunnery, as did Peter, a former abbot of Oliwa (1498–1500) at Żarnowiec (P). Bernard Iicha, monk of Vyšší Brod (C; *ob*. 1942), was provost of Porta Coeli (C), and when he died was buried there. A resident chaplain was a necessity, such as Michale le Cris, monk of Jardinet (B), and Augustine Truffler, monk of Vaucelles (F), who both served Marche-les-Dames (B) at different times, and John Scheider (*ob*. 1477), monk of Bronn-

---

[222] *NPRL*, pp. 216, 251; *NPRL2*, pp. 384, 587–8; *NPR*, pp. 642–3; *NKN*, p. 125.
[223] *NMD*, p. 156; *NGn*, p. 136.

bach, chaplain to the sisters of Frauental (Württemberg).[224] A confessor was also often resident, and on their deaths both chaplains and confessors were frequently buried in the nuns' cemetery, especially if their home monastery lay far distant.

Monks of Villers (B) were confessors at fourteen convents,[225] half of them in the province of Brabant, and four of which were founded under the aegis of Villers. Monks from St-Bernard-sur-l'Escaut (B) were confessors for the nuns of Herkenrode, Maagdendaal, Muysen, Nazareth, Roosendaal, Val-St-Bernard, Vrouenpark and Zwijeke. The necrology of Port-Royal (F) lists twenty-nine confessors between 1630 and 1706. One, Eustace (*ob.* 1716), a secular priest of the diocese of Lisieux, 'our confessor for eighteen years, was caught up in the Jansenist controversy of his time'. An *obit* list from Sonnenfeld names twelve chaplains serving the nunnery between 1276 and 1415, but not stating their own monastic house. At least one of the named chaplains of Gnadenthal was a monk of Schöntal.[226]

Confessors for Seligenthal (G) included Seyfrid Edelman (*ob.* 1440) from Kaisheim, and John Czabisch (*ob.* 1510), monk of Raitenhaslach (G), 'who

---

[224] *NOL*, p. 534; *NNC*, n.p; *NMD*, pp. 190, 188; *NFRW*, p. 48.
[225] Argenton, Binderen, Differdingen, Florival (Bloemendaal), Maagdendaal (Linter). Muizen, Nazareth, l'Olive, Rotem (Rothem), Terbeeck, Val-duc, Vrouenpark, Wauthier-Brain; *NV*, *passim*.
[226] *NBM*, *passim*; *NPRL*, pp. lxxi–lxxii; *NPRL2*, pp. 623–5; *NSN*, pp. 331–2; *NGn*, p. 138.

lives to God'. In 1508 a priest, Vitus, heard the confessions of the community, but then died, stricken by paralysis, and was buried at Seligenthal. Amongst its chaplains, at unknown dates, were George Rampslezhofer, Paul Sin and Bartholomew Höchenbarter, a monk of Raitenhaslach.[227] Other confessors included Nicholas (*ob*. 1602), monk of Ląd (P), for the nuns of Ołobok; Peter Heppeler, of Salem (A) at Heggbach; Wolfgang Geiger, monk of Langheim (G), 'a pious and zealous confessor' at Himmelkron (G); monks from Jardinet and Moulins for Marche-les-Dames, and from Camp and Val-Dieu for the nuns of Roermond. Maurice Bocheńska (*ob. c.*1740s), monk of Obra (P), died at Ołobok, where he was confessor.[228]

CONVERSI AND CONVERSAE

Given the large estates they frequently gained, and the everyday needs of a monastery, Cistercian monastic communities could not have survived without the support of bearded *conversi*, professed male religious who ate, slept and worshipped separately from the choir monks. In a sense they were lay brothers, but they were dismissive of that term. The *obit* list of Schönau (G) names two monks and one *conversus* who held the position of 'master of work'.[229]

---

[227] *NSA*, pp. 483, 481, 487, 501, 511.
[228] *NLA*, p. 476; *NSL*, p. 129; *NLH*, p. 295; *NMD*, pp. 181, 186, 188; *NRM*, pp. 8, 14.
[229] *NSC*, pp. 107–8.

Cistercian nunneries had a like body termed the *conversae*. Its necrology notes that Mary Mocqueux, a *conversa* of Marche-les-Dames, had been sixty-six years professed, and 'a boon to us'. At Baindt (G) Maria Catharine Wetlin (*ob.* 1700) was listed as a *conversa*, but later in the eighteenth century the term 'lay sisters' was used, as for Margaretha Veithin. At Billigheim (G) comes an undated reference to 'old Alheid, *conversa*'. At Frauenthal (Sw), dying around 1270, Ulric von Sedorf was a *conversus*, and his sister, Bertha, a *conversa*. At Owińska (P) Antonina (*ob.* 1772) was 'mistress of the *conversae*'.[230]

In the male Cistercian communities in the medieval period, until the Black Death, the numbers of *conversi* in a community frequently exceeded the number of its choir monks; they are not always reflected in the obituaries, perhaps because later compilers had no record of their existence, but, prior to 1402, the necrology of Pelplin (P) does note the *obits* of 146 *conversi* as opposed to 81 monks.[231]

The necrology of Ebrach (G) tells of the skills some *conversi* possessed. During the time of Abbot Alard (1238–?1244) the names of sixteen *conversi* as opposed to twenty-two monks are on record, including Wolfram, shoemaker, and Marquard, shepherd. During the time of Abbot Berthold (1252–63?) the names of thirty-five *conversi* are listed as opposed to those of

---

[230] *NMD*, p. 166; *NBT*, pp. 233, 238, 242; *NBH*, p. 58; *NFR*, p. 423; *NKN*, p. 60.
[231] *NPL, passim*.

twenty-eight monks, and included Henry, *conversus* in Salzheim; Henry, master of Herrnsdorf; Conrad in Dürrhof; Otto, tailor; Sifrid, baker; Henry, smith; Ludovic, shepherd; and Marquard, shoemaker; the places named were rural properties of the abbey.[232]

The obituary of Boneffe (B) records the deaths of eighty-four *conversi* between 1493 and 1722. Two were gardeners, one was a jubilarian; another, who met an untimely death, was a forester; another withdrew from his vocation and left the abbey in secular dress, yet was still remembered in its necrology. The skills of *conversi* were also evidenced by a list of 101 of those deceased at Zwettl (A), which included several with the occupations of 'snayter',[233] cook, gardener, shoe-maker, smith, mason, master of the brickyard and master of the wine.[234]

Of the nine *conversi* listed at Ebrach between 1714 and 1779, were those with the jobs of of sacristan, porter, blacksmith, and cabinet maker. One died from epilepsy, another from hydropsy. A manuscript list added to the rear fly-leaf of a volume concerning Ebrach notes the profession there of seven *conversi* and one oblate between the years 1727 and 1764.[235]

Other occupations which made Cistercian *conversi* a necessity to their communities included those of

---

[232] *NEBR*, p. 137.
[233] 'Snayter' occurs at least once as a Christian name in the USA, in 1802.
[234] *NBL*, pp. 263–4.
[235] *Brevia Notitia Monasterii Ebracensis*, Rome, 1739; *NEBR*, pp. 268–73.

almoner (Chunrad at Lilienfeld; A); archivist (Benedict Gamuths at Bronnbach; G); carpenter (Engelbert Widmar at Salem; A); cook (Dietmar at Wilhering; A); painter (Perthold at Lilienfeld); gardener (Balthasar Schiller, *ob.* 1804, at Salem); *grossmeister* (Heinrich, *ob.* 1280, at Frauenthal; Sw); guest-master (John Beck at Salem); porter (Jędrzejów, P); and shoe-maker (Laurence at Ląd, P, and Gerard at St-Bernard-sur-l'Escaut, B).[236]

Maurus Untersee (*ob.* 1773) at Salem was noted as 'a most expert and excellent smith'. Neuencamp (G) recorded the *obit* of Henning, 'who faithfully served us for thirty years'. At Wettingen (Sw) a monk, Wigand, was master of the *conversi*, as was a monk, Albert, at Bebenhausen (B) in 1271. At Ląd (P), in the late fifteenth century, comes mention of Dobersul, Dobrem and Reinard, 'semi-*conversi*'.[237]

Conversi might be tailors in their monastery, as was Udalric at Aldersbach (G), Walter at St-Bernard-sur-l'Escaut (B), Fabian Otto and Vitus Kügler at Kamieniec (P), and Alan Hoffmann at Paradyż (P). Aldersbach also made use of a lay tailor, Michael, 'who for many years served the monastery', and Raitenslach (G) had, as 'our tailor', Christan Hösinger, who died in 1473. At Pelplin (P), its lay tailor, Andrew Rautenstrauch, presented a black

---

[236] *NL*, p. 26; *NBR*, p. 108; *NSL*, p. 132; *NW*, p. 86; *NLD*, p. 372; *NSL*, p. 248, 221; *NFR*, p. 422; *NJD*, p. 778; *NLA*, p. 483; *NBM*, p. 101.
[237] *NSL*, p. 195; *NN*, p. 513; *NWT*, p. 592; *NBE*, p. 264; *NJD*, pp. 471, 492, 500.

chasuble to the abbey. Termed 'lay-brothers', Vincent Haller (*ob.* 1878) was a tailor at St Urban (Sw), and Anton Fellman (*ob.* 1883), a 'master tailor' there.[238]

The obituary of Bornem (B) tells of twelve of the *conversi* of Villers being sent in 1237 to found the first site of St-Bernard-sur-L'Escaut at Vremde, a suburb of Antwerp. They included Gerard, a gardener, William, a grange master, and Henry, a baker, the senior of the twelve. The community transferred to Hemiksem in 1246.[239]

FAMILIARS

These monastic assistants, usually resident in a monastery or on its granges, provided a variety of helpful services to a monastic community. They were layfolk, but were frequently accorded a distinctive garb, and a ceremony of admission. This is spelt out in the necrology of Boneffe (B), which makes it clear that, rather than being mere servants, they were enrolled as professed members of its household; the term used was 'familiar professed'. The roll of Boneffe includes the names of forty-seven familiars whose deaths occurred between 1483 and 1619. The death of two later familiars is noted: one in 1665 had acted as the porter of the abbey, and was described

---

[238] *NA*, p. 9; *NBM*, p. 90; *NKM*, images 12, 17; *NA*, p. 10; *NR*, p. 262; *NPL*, p. 112; *NSU*, p. 334.
[239] *NBM*, pp. 68–9, 163

as 'a perpetual familiar'. Another familiar was a jubilarian, and another, who passed away in 1780, was noted as being a tailor.[240] At the now Lutheran, but formerly Cistercian, monastery of Amelungsborn (G) today, in addition to the professed monks there is a body known as the the Bruderschaft or Familiaritas.[241] At Kamieniec (P) four familiars died between 1662 and 1666; three of them were women, one a man. The women presumably lived close by. A brother and sister, Michael and Margareth, were once both familiars there. One familiar of Kamieniec was the abbey archivist; Andrew, at Pelplin (P), was its shoe-maker; Laurence, at Jędrzejów (P), its organist. A female 'good familiar' of Lilienfeld (A) was one Alhayd, who served in the *domus peccatorum*; literally this means 'the house of sinners', but the correct transcription should probably be *domus pectorum*, 'the house of the carders of wool'.[242]

Some familiars were not penniless. The necrology of Neuencamp (G) tells of 'Ghezne Luttekens, our familiar, who for the remission of all his sins gave a pyx for the Body of Christ, one mark of pure silver, and an alb and amice'. At Boneffe, 'Peter van der Gheheucht (*ob.* 1568), familiar professed, was buried

---

[240] *NBN*, pp. 261, 294, 270, respectively.
[241] F. Gerhard, 'Kleine Chronik des Amelungsborne Familiaritas', in *Festschrift für Professor Karl Heinrich Rengstorf*, Berlin, 1963.
[242] *NKM*, images 8, 10, 20, 24, 26, 30; *NPL*, p. 74; *NJD*, p. 775; *NL*, p. 112, respectively.

in the village cemetery because of the burning of the monastery'.[243]

SERVANTS

The number of laymen and lay women earning wages from a monastic community, or at least their keep, rose over time as the numbers of *conversi* declined. Some servants stayed in the employ of Fürstenzell (G) for many years, including Nicholas, who had been 'a natural and laudable servant for forty years'. Hainrich Moliter, at Engelszell (A), had 'laboured effectively and faithfully for more than thirty years', whilst for the same monastery, Brigid (*ob.* 1497), 'our handmaid', had 'served the monastery faithfully for over thirty years'. The necrology of Lilienfeld (A) lauded Andrew Schuetenhelmer, 'who for over forty years laboured for the monastery, out of friendship, not only for food'.[244]

Some servants were waiters in a refectory, such as Adam Scloder at Fürstenzell (G), 'who daily faithfully and diligently served the community and ministered bread and drink, and also in winter-time looked after the calefactory with everything necessary' (i.e. when a fire was lit). At Lilienfeld (A) Chunigund of Vienna 'for many years served us bread and wine in the chamber'. At Wilhering (A) Levtold of Chirberg

---

[243] *NN*, p. 515; *NBN*, p. 264, respectively.
[244] *NF* 118; *NE*, pp. 254, 256; *NLD*, p. 413, respectively.

was 'a very capable soldier, who served us both at breakfast and supper'.[245]

Servants might include a baker (such as John Franck at Raitenhaslach, G); a balneator (such as Liebhard at Engelszell, A); a blacksmith (such as John Lindemayr at Fürstenzell, G); a brewer (such as Mikula at Ląd and John at Pelplin, P); a calefactor (such as Christlin at Wilhering);[246] a carpenter (such as Stephen Mendel at Ląd); a cook (such as John Hoffman at Kamieniec, P); a courier (such as Herman at Raitenhaslach); a farm labourer (such as Innocent Fai, *ob.* 1660, at Port-Royal, F), 'a faithful and pious servant who tilled the land, and looked after the horses'; a fisherman (such as Andrew at Fürstenzell);[247] a guest-master (such as George Chûestainer at Raitenhaslach); a hair dresser (*triciator*, such as Drabo at Pelplin); or an inn-keeper (*caupo*, such as Ulrich, *ob.* 1488, at Wilhering).[248]

Others might be a kitchen servant (such as Wölfin, also at Wilhering); a master of the cess pit (such as John of Rynoy, *ob.* 1399, at St Servaas, Utrecht); a miller (such as Martin at Ląd); a rope maker (such as John at Wilhering); a shoe-maker (such as Leonhard, at Wilhering); and a tailor (such as Laurence at Fürstenzell).[249] Amongst the servants and officers of

---

[245] *NF*, p. 107; *NLD*, p. 380.
[246] *NR*, p. 269; *NF*, p. 122; *NLA*, p. 475; *NPL*, p. 82; *NW*, p. 75.
[247] *NLD*, p. 390; *NPRL*, p. 19; *NF*, p. 117.
[248] *NR*, p. 273; *NPL*, p. 75; *NWL*, p. 446; '*caupo* at the gate' at Rein: *NRE*, p. 351.
[249] *NWL*, p. 447; *NSS*, p. 130; *NLA*, p. 484; *NW*, pp. 133, 87; *NF*,

Spiritual Fraternity

Seligenthal (Landshut) nunnery over the years were: an architect, a baker, 'chursenmaister', a kitchen master, a 'master of the premises', a procurator, scribes, a shoe-maker, and a weaver. There was also a skinner, Henry; he, and his father, were both *conversi* there.[250] A few servants saved enough money to bequeath a gift to their monastery: George Lockner (*ob*. 1619), cook at Bronnbach (G), left it 100 French florins; John, brewer at Pelplin, left the abbey 490 florins; Martin, baker at Jędrzejów (P), 'out of his wages' gave the abbey ten marks to purchase a chasuble and other vestments.[251] As for the monastic habits, Countess Elizabeth of Scharberch, noted as foundress, gave Wilhering black cowls, whilst Stams (A) was left 'an annual gift for all time of black cloth for making cowls'.[252] *Conversi* tailors included Fabian Otto and Vitus Kügler at Kamieniec (P), and John at Ląd, and amongst lay tailors Christan Hösinger (*ob*. 1473) supplied the needs of Raitenhaslach, and one, Michael, 'for many years served the needs of Aldersbach'.[253]

SPIRITUAL FRATERNITY

A monastic community might enter into a bond of fellowship with individuals, often benefactors,

---

p. 111.
[250] *NSA, passim*.
[251] *NBR*, p. 136; *NPL*, p. 82; *NJD*, p. 787.
[252] *NW*, p. 115; *NST*, wp. 48.
[253] *NKM*, images 12, 17; *NLA*, p. 483; *NR*, p. 262; *NA*, p. 10.

or with one or more other religious communities, which mutually promised each other a share in their 'matins, the hours, Masses, vespers, vigils, prayers and other spiritual benefits'. At the nunnery of Baindt (G), 22 June was kept as a commemoration of all those deceased 'who had held fraternity with us'. At Salem (A), 17 June was observed in commemoration of its benefactors and those in fraternity. The necrology of Roermond makes repeated note of 'the fraternity of the Blessed Virgin Mary', and of grants made to it, but perhaps these refer to the community itself.[254]

The necrology of St Servaas, Utrecht, appends two lists of those in fraternity, the second being of donors to the cost of windows in its refectory. A list from Lilienfeld (A) names 118 persons in fraternity. An appendix to the necrology of Seligenthal (Landshut, G) names some twenty clerics and over fifty lay individuals in fraternity. It enjoyed mutual fraternity with the monastery of Kaisheim (G), but suprisingly there is no mention of Raitenhaslach (A), with which it had close associations. Koronowo (P) lists twenty-three individuals and four religious congregations as being its *confratres* and *consorores*.[255]

The obituary of Altenberg (G) has constant references to the deceased religious of the Austrian Benedictine house of Göttweig, suggesting that the two

---

[254] E.g. NPR, pp. 638, 641; NBT, p. 237; NSL p. 166; NRM, *passim*.
[255] NSS, *passim*; NSA, pp. 520–1; NL, pp. 186, 188; NKN, pp. 145–7.

Spiritual Fraternity

monasteries had entered into a bond of fraternity. Abbot Burchard Iselin of Tennenbach (G; *ob.* ?1452) arranged spiritual confraternity for his community with the Cistercian nuns of Günterstal (G). The nuns of Marche-les-Dames (B) enjoyed fraternity with the Crucifers (Crutched Friars) and canons of the Holy Cross at nearby Huy, listing in total 114 of them. The necrology of Kamieniec (P) names five canons regular of Kłodzko as *confratres*, at least two of them dying in 1521; was that a consequence of local troubles?[256]

Jędrzejów (P) had 135 male *confratres* and 58 female *confratrices*, mostly of laity, but there were included two hermits, a nun of the Order of St Norbert and a Franciscan friar. The community also enjoyed fraternity with the Order of St Paul, the First Hermit, arranged with its prior-general, Martin Gruszkowicz (*ob.* 1635). Of the male *confratres* nine were goldsmiths of different periods, mostly based in Kraków. Servants might also be *confratres*, such as Albert de Piędziczow, the monastery's cook at an unknown date. John Otreba (*ob.* 1430), a *confrater*, gave the abbey thirty Polish marks 'and other things'.[257]

Bishop William de Rale of Winchester (E) was received into fraternity in 1446 by Wintney nunnery (E). Fürstenzell (G) kept the *obit* of the parents of a *confrater*, Thomas Chümerl of Passau, one of fourteen siblings. At Soleilmont (B), Jean d'Ardenos

---

[256] NAL, pp. 339–44; NT, p. 338; NMD, *passim*; NKM, images 45, 47, 51.
[257] NJD, pp 774, 784, 794–801.

Cistercian Chronicles and Necrologies

(*ob.* 1567) gave the nuns 120 florins 'for participation in our prayers'.[258] At Lilienfeld, Wysento, 'formerly of Neuenburg, who has fraternity with us, became our special friend'. At Kamieniec, a former sawyer of the abbey, John Bonumgarten, was received into fraternity. AtLąd the reciprocity was give to Archdeacon Vincent Łagiewnicki of Gniezno, whilst a *consoror* there, Anna Wardęska (*ob.* 1678), was said to be 'of optimum merit'.[259]

THE INFIRMARIES AND THE SICK

Sick religious were cared for in the infirmary, which could become inadequate in time. Its necrology reveals Abbot Henry of Altenberg (G; *ob.* 1327) as the 'founder' of its infirmary, but clearly replacing an earlier edifice. The fifty-eighth abbot of Villers (B), Jacques Hache (1716–34), rebuilt the infirmary, whilst in 1790 a new infirmary was constructed at Ebrach (G). A monastic infirmary usually had a chapel attached, such as that built at Heiligenkreuz by Archduke Albert I of Austria (1298–1308). At Pairis (F) an infirmary chapel was dedicated in 1325 'in honour of St Thomas of Canterbury, St Gregory, and St Peter, archbishop of Tarentaise (*ob.* 1174)', a Cistercian concerned for the poor and the ill.[260]

---

[258] *NWN*, p. 390; *NF*, p. 113; *NSO*, p. 390.
[259] *NLD*, p. 381; *NKM*, image 58; *NLA*, pp. 471, 491.
[260] *NAL*, p. 342; *NV*, p. 71; *NEBR*, p. 302; *NH*, pp. 114–15; *NPS*, p. 86.

The Infirmaries and the Sick

In charge was a monk, 'master of the infirmary', such as Sebastian (*ob.* 1530) at Bronnbach (G); Wolfgang (*ob.* 1480) at Rein (A); Christian (*ob.* 1617) at Salem (A); and Hainrich at Lilienfeld (A), where Nicholas was the infirmary cook.[261] A layman at Pelplin (P) was John Fullenbrock (*ob.* 1594), 'who from adolescence until the age of ninety years faithfully served our infirmary'. At Salem *conversi* served as apothecaries, such as Modest Rösel (*ob.* 1741) and Norbert Hoffmann (*ob.* 1778), but so too did a monk, Damian Schmid (*ob.* 1754). At Oliwa (P), Gregory Postki (*ob.* 1724), a *conversus*, was both 'infirmary attendant and apothecary'. At Stams (A) Hanns Peck had been 'faithful servant of the infirm'.[262]

A 'lay *conversus*' of Bronnbach, Barabas Keller (*ob.* 1824), was a surgeon. External surgeons were called if the need arose. The obituary of Pelplin records the *obits* of 'Joachin Posselum (*ob.* 1625), doctor of Gdańsk, for many years our familiar and medical man', and of Peter Grunwalt (*ob.* 1629), 'our surgeon for many years, who left us more than one hundred florins'.[263] Rein had Henry, 'medical man, deacon'. At Ląd (P), Casimir Swierkiewicz (*ob.* 1692), was noted as 'our servant, a surgeon of optimum merit'.[264]

Alcohol was seen as helpful for the sick. Ebrach in 1150 received a grant of white wine 'for those

---

[261] NBR, p. 113; NRE, p. 352; NLD, pp. 411, 415.
[262] NPL, p. 90; NSL, pp. 283, 76, 77; NOL2, p. 147; NST, p. 554.
[263] NBR, p. 132; NPL, pp. 80, 88.
[264] NRE, p. 342; NLA, p. 487 (*famulus*, 'servant').

weakened when bled', a procedure carried out in the calefactory. Mathias Cannengeter gave the monks of Neuencamp a tun of beer to drink, and another 'for the infirmary'. Engelszell received a gift from Alheid of a vineyard to cater for the needs of the infirm, and Anne of Wienne gave Lilienfeld a vineyard 'for wine in the infirmary on St Clement's Day' (23 November).[265]

Perchtade Neuberg donated to Wilhering a vineyard for its infirmary, and its necrology notes that on 9 August, 'those in the infirmary are served with fish and white bread'. It also tells of two leprous monks.[266] Other gifts for the infirmary at Lilienfeld included ten florins for a light in the infirmary, 'proper provision' on St Catherine's Day (25 November), and by 1480, two vessels and two couches.[267]

FOOD SUPPLY

The early White Monks, if healthy, abstained from flesh-meat,[268] which made *fish* significant in their diet, and most abbeys lay by a river or lake. Necrologies relate that Newminster (E) had three fisheries in the River Tyne, whilst Pelplin (P) was given Lake Bobancyn. Otto Pistoris and his wife donated a fishery

---

[265] *NEBR*, p. 133; *NN*, pp. 512–13, *NE*, p. 254; *NLD*, p. 421.
[266] *NWL*, p. 445; *NW*, pp. 147, 163.
[267] *NLD*, pp. 421, 426, respectively.
[268] Wilhering had a 'piggery', served by laymen: Martin, Mertlin (*ob*. 1480), and John: *NW*, pp. 96, 135; *NWL*, p. 456.

Food Supply

at Hergoltingen to Kaisheim (G), whilst Conrad of Wildenrod gave Fürstenfeld (G) a herring fishery at Puech, herring being much eaten by the Cistercians in Advent and Lent.[269] Udalric of Leuwolfing gave Aldersbach (G) a fishery in Brunne, 'from which fish were provided for the community on the four feasts of the Blessed Virgin Mary, and on his anniversary'. The monks of Lilienfeld (A) each received, as part of an undated grant, 'a piece of fish for the solace of the community', whilst an annual grant of three measures of wheat from Raseldorf (presumably to be sold) were to provide for its community to have fish at supper.[270]

An undated bequest made to Salem (A) by a novice priest of twenty pounds was to be divided between the need for clothes and the purchase of fish, whilst on the *obit* (25 August) of a duke of Lower Bavaria, a pittance of fish was to be provided by the bursar. Cambron (B) employed a fisherman by the name of Osto de la Warde (*ob.* 1539), whilst Pelplin kept the *obit* of 'Bernard, our fisherman, who for many years served the monastery faithfully'; Fürstenzell (G) observed that of Andrew, one of its fishermen; Heiligenkreuz (A) that of Thomas, a fisherman, and Neuencamp (G) that of Gregory Werneke, 'master of our fishery'.[271]

---

[269] *NNM*, p. 401; *NPL*, p. 65; *NKH*, p. 91; *NFN*, p. 98.
[270] *NA*, p. 14; *NLD*, p. 423;
[271] *NSL*, pp. 195, 223; *NL*, p. 132; *NC*, p. 116; *NPL*, p. 82; *NF*, p. 117; *NH*, p. 112; *NN*, p. 514.

Another necessity was the provision of *salt*. The necrology of Aldersbach (G) tells us that an unnamed duke of Bavaria allowed its monks 'to take salt freely in Burckhausen and Schärding', whilst Engelszell (A) had liberty of salt at Eno (from Prince Stephen of Hungary, *ob.* 1606), and at Gmünden (from Queen Elizabeth of the Romans; *ob.* 1308).[272]

Duke Henry III of Bavaria (*ob.* 1290), 'under whom the monastery was founded', granted Fürstenzell 'fifty large vessels (*cuppas*) of salt, called Muezsalcz. The obituary of Wilhering (A), under the date of 2 May 1312, instructed that 'on the first vacant day after the feast of Ss Philip and James [1 May], the anniversary was to be kept of Duke Albert I of Austria (*ob.* 1 May 1308), and Elizabeth his wife, and for all dukes of Austria, who gave us annually thirty weights (*pondera/fueder*) of salt of Halstatt'. Lilienthal received a measure of salt from a priest, Conrad Talakren.[273]

Necrologies relate that monks might be 'masters of the bakehouse', as at Aldersbach (G) and Oliwa (P), or else *conversi*, as at Neuencamp (G). A monk, Ulrich Sattler, was baker of Salem (A) for more than thirty years.[274] At Pelplin (P), John (*ob.* 1644), '*conversus* and baker', was able (perhaps on admission) to give his abbey over 2,000 florins. Servants in the bakery might be male, as Leonard at Aldersbach,

---

[272] *NA*, p. 18; *NE*, pp. 241, 245.
[273] *NF*, p. 108; *NW*, p. 87; *NTK*, p. 530.
[274] *NA*, pp. 11, 15: *NOL*, p. 507; *NN*, p. 517; *NSL*, p. 3.

Food Supply

or female in later years, like Richeldis at Lilienfeld, who gave 'eighteen years of faithful service in the bakehouse'.[275]

Flour came from the granarian, such as Christopher at Aldersbach, 'prior, and keeper for a long time of the granary', or Jacob Bal (*ob.* 1704), jubilarian at St-Bernard-sur-l'Escaut (B); or from a sub-prior, such as Adam Seifridt (*ob.* 1639) at Langheim (G); or from a layman, such as George Schrom (*ob.* 1667) at Kamieniec (P), 'granarian, and faithful servant of the monastery'. At Wilhering Ulrich was a 'servant of the granary'.[276] Grants of mills are noted in the necrologies, as for Orval (B) at Herbuval and Molines, and of Wald (G) at Hedwang, as also are the names of millers: Cuthbert, *conversus*, of Fürstenzell (G); Otto, a lay miller for Wilhering; and, at Kamieniec (P), Susanna Bausin (*ob.* 1678), 'miller in the new mill'.[277]

Orval received four grants of spelt, forty-six measures in all, a grain seen as a health food, whilst John of Luxembourg, king of Bohemia (*ob.* 1356), bequeathed an annual grant of six measures of razed spelt to Marche-les-Dames. The nunnery was also bequeathed in total in succession about 200 measures of spelt by the parents of Joan Hodge, one of its nuns, and by a benefactor who died in 1621 'one

---

[275] *NPL*, p.94; *NA*, p. 10;
[276] *NA*, p. 9; *NBM*, p. 82; *NLC*, p. 289; *NKM*, image 6; *NWL*, p. 446.
[277] *NO*, p. 224; *NWD*, p. 218; *NF*, p. 112; *NW*, p. 166; *NKM*, image 4.

measure of spelt for our recreation on the vigil of St Giles' (31 August).[278]

Monastic cooks have been noted, such as Dietmar, *conversus* and cook at Wilhering. Salem had a kitchener and a sub-kitchener, monk and *conversus*: James Mader (*ob.* 1637) and Gervase Feuchtmayr (*ob.* 1738). The obituary of Kamieniec notes the *obits* of Christopher and Gregory, monks, and 'prefects of the kitchen', and on its staff at one time, 'Katherine, cook and servant'. The mortuary book of Koronowo (P) tells of a *conversus*, Mathias Patritius Koziński (*ob.* 1767), as prefect of its kitchen. The necrology of Aldersbach notes Peter Lenawer, 'old and faithful servant of the kitchen'.[279]

For the conveyance of food, and travel by abbots and cellarers, horses were important. Fürstenfeld (G) received 'three horses with their trappings'; Pelplin, four horses (from Arnold of Lichtenow); Wettingen (Sw), 'a large horse with trappings (from Count John of Hapsburg; *ob.* 1337); Wilhering, two horses (from Erdinger of Wels); and Neuburg (G), two horses, one valued at ten florins, and the other at twenty-six marks.[280] Engleszell (A) praised on his *obit* 'Caspar, our faithful stableman', and Fürsten-

---

[278] *NO*, pp. 224–8; *NMD*, pp. 305, 169, 309.
[279] *NWL*, p. 454; *NSL*, pp. 4, 106; *NKM*, images 17, 7; *NKN*, p. 150; *NA*, p. 18.
[280] *NA*, p. 8; *NFN*, p. 103; *NWT*, p. 595; *NW*, p. 94; *NN*, pp. 511, 514.

zell lauded Andrew Krentholm (*ob.* 1481), 'our very faithful servant and stableman'.[281]

There is scant mention of orchards in the necrologies, but Wilhering (A) received a gift of two, and at Salem (A) Ulrich, a *conversus*, was fruiterer.[282] Wine could be a source of income, as well as safe to drink. The necrology of Lilienfeld (A) tells of thirty vineyards donated to the monastery—one of them to provide 'honest service' for the community on the feast of Ss Abdon and Sennen (30 July), whilst that of Wilhering records twelve, two of them devoted to the well-being of the infirm.[283] It was noted of Pairis (F) that Ulrich of Keiserperg (*ob.* 1316) 'gave us many vineyards in Amerswilre', and at Heiligenkreuz (A) Duke Henry of Metildich gave the abbey seven vineyards, whilst Engelszell (A) received thirteen, two for the use of the sub-cellarer, one for 'the chamber' and one for the infirmary. Seligenthal (G) received 'an urn of good wine' yearly on 25 January.[284]

Preuilly (F) received, close to its Maloreposte Grange, 'land for the planting of vines'. At Lilienfeld (A) the necrology takes note of Peter Walkhayme, 'our faithful vine dresser at Neuwuerga', and of Gerius, 'paid helper and good assistant of our vineyard in Racleinsstorf'. One Heinrich was vinedresser at Raitenhaslach (G), and a monk of Salem, Quirinius Gindelin (*ob.* 1574), bore the title of *vinitor*,

---

[281] *NE*, p. 257; *NF*, p. 123.
[282] *NW*, p. 88, 151; *NSL*, p. 4 (*pomerius*).
[283] *NLD*, *passim*; *NW*, *passim*.
[284] *NPS*, p. 72; *NH*, p. 110; *NE*, *passim* and p. 243; *NSA*, p. 476.

perhaps having entire charge of the abbey's viticulture. In cooler northen climes beer was significant, and the obituary of Neuencamp (G) tells of the grant by different donors of eleven tuns of beer for the community to drink, or cash to buy them, with a further tun for the use of the infirmary.[285]

PITTANCES

The spartan diet of the Cistercians became in time more luxurious as grants were made, especially for *obit* days, of money to support the cost of an extra dish of food, or a glass of better wine, to be served to a community; such grants were referred to as 'pittances' or 'services'. For these purposes a monk held the office of pitancier, as at Bebenhausen (G) and Lilienfeld (A); otherwise, the sub-prior or the sub-cellarer might fulfil this role. A nun, Katherine Rubsin (*ob.* 1431), was the 'pittance mistress' at Frauental (Württemberg).[286]

Some monasteries enjoyed many days with a pittance; the nuns of Baindt (G) over its six-hundred-year history accrued over one hundred pittances of wine each year, the monks of Wilhering seventy-six, and the monks of Orval twenty-nine daily pittances in the short period between 1 March and 26 July. The

---

[285] *NP*, p. 85; *NLD*, pp. 40, 410; *NR*, p. 264; *NSL*, p. 284; *NN*, pp. 512–17.
[286] *NBE*, p. 273; *NLD*, p. 395; *NFRW*, p. 45.

nuns of Roermond (H) had each year 135 pittances of wine, in addition to several days of 'solemn service', and of 'wheaten bread' on Maundy Thursday.[287]

Wald (G) had sixteen pittances recorded, or the money to cover their cost; at Preuilly one bequest was of fifty shillings for the provision of a pittance. Notre-Dame-des-Prés (F) in its obituary had twenty-two, mostly in value ranging from 20 to 60 shillings to defray their cost. John of Chanoy and Joan, his wife, bequeathed to Marche-les-Dames (B) six Holland *oboli*, two for their anniversaries, and four 'for the recreation of the community on the day of anniversary, inviting close blood relatives or friends'.[288]

The monks of Du Val (F) received cash to cover the cost of pittances. Its necrology states that William of Ormetiaux, esquire, gave twenty shillings for a pittance there on his *obit* (22 July), and, further, on the anniversary of the death of Queen Blanche (22 February), 'that we ought to have twenty-four shillings for a pittance'. Emilius of Mniden (*ob.* 1482) gave annually to the sisters of St Servaas, Utrecht, 'three gold coins, in memory of his wife and daughter, from which we buy a pint of wine for each sister', whilst the mother of 'our nun Gertrude' provided 'for each nun wine three times in the year'. The nuns of the abbey also received pittances of malmsey and on two occasions a *menghel* for each nun.[289]

---

[287] *NBT, passim; NW, passim; NO, passim; NRM, passim* and p.19.
[288] *NWD, passim; NP,* p. 883; *NDP, passim; NMD,* p. 188.
[289] *NVA,* pp. 630–1; *NSS,* pp. 107, 139, 136, 163, 112, 148; *menghel*

Some pittances granted were intended to vary monastic diet during the two fasting seasons of Advent and Lent. Lilienfeld (A) received a gift of Gegenler vineyard 'for the solace of the convent in Advent', whilst Nicholas of Wildungsmauer (A) gave the monastery a pittance on Ash Wednesday. A similar grant was made to Rein (A), and for the following day. The residue of a grant provided Orval (B) with dried herrings for Advent and Lent, whilst another donor provided 16 lb of almonds for Lent.[290]

Jardin (F) was bequeathed ten pounds for a pittance 'at the coming of Lent'.[291] The monks of Kaisheim (G) received income from a knight, Kunon of Kullingen, 'who in agony received our habit', providing 'olive oil and herrings in Lent' (this clause reminds us that some benefactors in the earlier Middle Ages chose to die clothed as monks). At the beginning of Advent, Aldersbach (G) benefited from property given to it at Hochlols, 'allowing a pittance to be served on the fourth day before the feast of St Nicholas' (i.e. on 2 December). The necrology of Billigheim (G) notes five donors for the same day, 'in the advent of Our Lord', who between them gave its nuns for this season five urns of wine.[292]

A fragmentary table tells of the 'services' to be provided at Wilhering (A) on specified days. These

was an old standard measure for liquids, but the text here does not say which drink was envisaged.
[290] NLD, pp. 402, 376; NRE, p. 343; NO, pp. 229–30.
[291] NJ, p. 433: 'In adventu quadragesima'.
[292] NKH, p. 91; NA, p. 25; NBH, p. 62.

Pittances

included Laetare Sunday (Lent 4) and the two days following, the feast of Dedication, and even Monday in Holy Week (these pittances frequently consisting of 'fish and white bread'); and the feasts of St John before the Latin Gate (6 May), and of St Pancratius (12 May). A donor of Aldersbach granted it two courts (granges) in Pachhausen and Perwing, and a fishery at Brunne, 'from which are administered fish and flour and good wine on the four feasts of the Blessed Virgin Mary, and on his anniversary'.[293]

Aldersbach (G) also had a pittance provided for it by Margaret Erlbechkin, prioress of Altach, on the feast of Corpus Christi, whilst Fürstenzell (G) was granted a rent of one talent at Hunthauppen to allow on his *obit* day a pittance for the community of 'good fish, white bread, and good wine'. The nuns of Marche-les-Dames (B) were bequeathed by their porter, who died in 1602, seven *oboli* 'for good wine on Christmas Day'. The nuns of Billigheim (G) received a grant of six white loaves.[294]

The fragmentary necrology of Heilsbronn tells of thirty-five pittances received between the months of May and August, mostly of 'fish, bread and wine'. Some were for specified feasts or other liturgical days, as 'the third feria in the rogation days' (i.e. Rogation Wednesday); 'the feast of Pentecost' (by grant of Bishop Bertold of Würzburg), and 'the Friday after the octave of Pentecost'. Fish on Fridays in

---

[293] *NW*, pp. 64–74, 106, 124; *NA*, p. 14.
[294] *NA*, p. 16; *NF*, p. 120; *NMD*, p. 307; *NBH*, p. 66.

summer was listed against the anniversary of Walburg of Vendebach.[295]

Neuencamp (G) was granted pittances totalling twenty-eight marks on the feasts of Penteost, the Holy Trinity and Corpus Christi. Wald (G) at each feast of Corpus Christi received *Allwegen* by bequest of Margaret and Osanna von Ryschach, and on Ascension Day a gift of twenty florins annually. The monks of Stams (A) received a grant to provide white bread 'in value one *grossus* at least' around the feast of All Saints each year.[296]

Highly prized in Cistercian diet were eggs. A gift to the monks of Orval (B) included the cost of three eggs daily per monk from Pentecost to the Assumption (15 August), and from Holy Cross Day (14 September) through to All Saints' Day (1 November). A like grant for Lilienfeld (A) derived from its Schilpach grange 'three eggs which are ministered to us from Trinity Sunday to Holy Cross Day'. A substantial bequest allowed eggs for the monks of Heilsbronn in the forenoon throughout the summer. Arnold, master of the imperial chamber, gave Fürstenfeld (G) an annuity for eggs, whilst for Aldersbach, 'Reinhard, formerly a parish priest of St Paul in Passau, but now a novice here, provided for the cellarer to minister to us a third egg at supper on fast days'.[297]

---

[295] *NHB, passim*, especially pp. 126–9: Berthold I was bishop from 1271 to 1274; Berthold II from 1274 to 1287.
[296] *NN*, pp. 510–11; *NWD*, p. 219; *NST*, p. 57.
[297] *NO*, pp. 239, 236; *NLD*, p. 420; *NHB*, p. 127: 'mane in prandio' (? breakfast'); *NFN*, p. 98; *NA*, p. 21.

The Granges and Monastic Villages

THE GRANGES AND MONASTIC VILLAGES

The backbone of the food supply of the Cistercians were their farms (termed 'granges' or 'courts'), where the labour force (the *conversi* and lay workers) lived, with the usual buildings of barns, dwelling accommodation and an oratory.

Granges might be received as a gift, as when King Chunrad of the Romans granted Gaistal and Werndorf to Rein (A), and when Berchtold Purger gave its court at Michelskirchen to Fürstenfeld (G). Benefactors might receive burial in a monastery they had favoured: James of Cons, who gifted Caure Grange to Orval (B), was interred close to its chapter-house; Conrad Hübschwirt, who granted its court at Ysenwang to Fürstenfeld, was buried at the abbey close to the altar of St James.[298]

A grange or entire village might be bought: gifts of 100 and 45 sexagenas respectively enabled Vyšší Bród (C) to purchase its villages of Swynyehlawa and Okole. Granges might be exchanged for others more conveniently placed: Newminster (E) received property at Ruthlan in exchange for territory at Cambron, and it exchanged its Caldewell grange for lands in Clifton. Granges might be extended, as when the monks of Preuilly (F) received 'land for the planting of vines' close to a grange.[299]

---

[298] *NRE*, p. 343; *NFN*, p. 97, *NO*, p. 225; *NFN*, p. 97.
[299] *NHN*, pp. 384–5; *NNM*, pp. 401–2; *NP*, p. 85

In charge of a grange would normally be a 'procurator' or 'provost'. For Salem's (A) property at Schemmerburg, a monk, Anthony of Alltmannshausen (*ob.* 1691), had charge for 'twenty-one laudable years', and later another monk, Robert Adam (*ob.* 1755) was provost there. Distance from the abbey meant that on their deaths both were buried where they served. For more than forty years, 'H', a *conversus*, was the 'master' of Salem's (A) property at Leutkich, whilst for some time, a *conversus*, Hainrich, was 'master of our court' in Radebrunn for Lilienfeld (A).[300]

The necrology of Langheim (G) lists eighteen 'provisors' in charge of its court at Tambach beween 1356 and 1476 and from 1525 to 1663, eleven of whom in the latter period may have been lay officials. Likewise, from the sixteenth century onwards lay officials appear among the eleven named provisors at Culmbach. Occasionally the obituaries mention others who staffed these rural courts, such as Margareth (*ob.* 1702), a familiar at Kamieniec's (P) property in Franskensteyn, and Wilhering's (A) 'faithful servant', Henry Homerl, at Eyttenpers. At an unknown date, and somewhat surprisingly, one Elizabeth was named as Rein's (A) procurator at Strazsindel.[301]

An oratory or chapel was a focus of worship at most, if not all, granges. Its necrology notes some of those of Pairis (F), which had a chapel dedicated to

---

[300] *NSL*, pp. 322, 325 284; *NL*, p. 68.
[301] *NLH, passim*; *NKM*, image51; *NW*, p. 75; *NRE*, p. 352.

The Granges and Monastic Villages

St Anthony at Widen grange; another in honour of Our Lady at Hohnaea; and a chapel dedicated in 1391 to Ss Bartholomew and Bernard 'at our court in Kaiserperg'. At its Buch grange (St Barbara's grange), a chapel with three altars was dedicated on Holy Cross Day (14 September 1474), in honour of St Barbara, St John the Evangelist and Ss Sebastian and Anthony.[302]

Monks frequently served village churches granted to their abbey: at Allersheim, some 230 km north of Bronnbach (G), amongst other religious, Sebastian Udalric (*ob.* 1627), a former abbot, and Hermann Volker (*ob.* 1731) and Engelbert Meisner (*ob.* 1799), monks of the house, served as the parish priest. When they died the great distance to their monastery at Bronnbach meant that they were buried at Allersheim.[303]

A major property of Kamieniec was at Wartha,[304] now known as Bardo, and in Cistercian hands from 1299 to 1810, with a new church that the abbot had built in 1421. Over the years it had a whole range of monks from the abbey serving it, such as John Labrisser (*ob.* 1680), 'once provost'; Christian Lorenz (*ob.* 1757), 'once superior'; Jacob Lew (*ob.* 1457), 'once prefect'; and Dominic, sub-superior in 1733.[305]

Chaplains are noted, such as John Baptist Böhmer (*ob.* 1715), and Peter, formerly prior at Kamie-

---

[302] *NPS*, pp. 85, 87, 89; *NPS1*, p. 60.
[303] *NBR*, pp. 106, 97.
[304] See also T. Halusa, 'Eine Vergissmeinnicht für Wartha und Camenz', *Cistercienser-Chronik* 7, no. 75, May 1895.
[305] *NKM*, images 9, 16, 56, 25, 31.

niec. Frequent mention is made of monks acting as penitentiaries at Wartha, including Ambrose Scrieff (*ob.* 1723), and Charles Langer (*ob.* 1732), 'penitentiary and preacher'.[306] The necrology lists Herman, at unknown date, as being the abbey's fisherman in Wartha. It also tells that, close to Wartha, Abbot Tobias of Kamieniec died unexpectedly on Holy Saturday morning in 1757.[307]

URBAN PROPERTY

Athough themselves situated in relatively remote locations, many Cistercian monasteries owned major dwellings in a nearby town or city. Described as their 'house', 'court' or 'refuge' in that place, these made for easy access to the local bishop, provided a residence for monks studying at a local college or on business, and importantly facilitated trade in their monastery's produce. In times of local disturbances, they might well indeed be safe havens for the monks.

Monasteries might own many other dwellings in an urban setting, gaining income from their rents. Preuilly (F) was once awarded the rent valued at twenty pounds arising from a number of houses in Forgerii Street in Paris. It also had 'our large house in Paris' there, which had been given it by a former monk of Preuilly, Walter (*ob.* 1231), bishop of Char-

---

[306] *NKM*, images 3, 62, 17, 28.
[307] *NKM*, images 45, 19.

Urban Property

tres.[308] A town dwelling might also make a suitable retirement home. The thirty-seventh abbot of Cambron (B), now aged seventy-eight, died 'at our refuge in Ath', the local cathedral city. A nun of Port-Royal-des-Champs (F), Marie-Angelique (*ob.* 1641), died at its house in Paris.[309]

The city of Krems in Austria had a strong Cistercian presence; their obituaries show that Engelszell, Fürstenzell, Raitenhaslach and Wilhering all had a 'court' there. Such city dwellings needed an administrator and servants. The necrologies give few dates, but they do tell that at one time a monk of Wilhering, John Kirichmair, was 'provisor' of its house in Krems, and Siboto, a faithful servant there. Engelszell had a 'driver' or 'waggoner' (*auriga*) attached to its house in Krems—perhaps a sign of the conveyance of goods, and Raitenhaslach a female servant, Elizabeth.[310]

As with the chaplaincies and granges, a resident monk on his demise might well be buried locally. The obituary of Fürstenzell tells of Stephen Hubschmann (*ob.* 1467), 'monk, who died at our court in Krems, and is buried at the preachers there', i.e. at the local Dominican friary.[311]

Amongst the monks placed by Boneffe (B) at its property in Namur were Joachim Bormans (*ob.* 1651), 'in charge of our refuge in Namur', and Leonard Laumonie (*ob.* 1715), 'in charge of our hospice in

---

[308] *NP*, pp. 884, 887.
[309] *NC*, p. 123; *NPRL2*, p. 180.
[310] *NW*, pp. 102, 165; *NE*, p. 258; *NR*, p. 282.
[311] *NF*, p. 123.

Namur'. For Salem (A), Conrad Erfranck (*ob.* 1498), monk, was 'a faithful procurator in Eslingen', and Conrad Schwartz (*ob.* 1662), monk, 'a laudable administrator and procurator of our house in Überlingen'. For Raitenhaslach (G), Conrad, monk, was 'our guest-master (*hospes*) in Stams'.[312]

A series of monks managed Bronnbach's 'court' in Würzburg, where an image of Our Lady stood in the courtyard.[313] Lay officers noted in its necrology included Henry, Nicholas and Wernhard, at different times house-keeper or guest-master for Engelszell (A) in Passau. Siffrid Müller served in the same capacity for Kaisheim (G) at Lauingen. Monks took charge of the house of Bebenhausen (G) in Stuttgart, and its hospital in Tübingen.[314]

The necrology of Villers (B) tells how 'during the time of the fifty-fifth abbot, Thomas Maniot (*ob.* 1697), many miseries afflicted our house of Villers, among which was the total destruction by fire of our hospice in Brussels'. His successor, Anthony Pinchart, started the work of restoration, and later the sixty-second abbot, Robert de Bavoy (abbot, 1765–82), 'adorned our refuge at Brussels, inside and outside, splendidly and sumptuously'.[315]

---

[312] *NBN*, pp. 278–9, 289; *NSL*, pp. 106, 109; *NR*, p. 280.
[313] *NBR, passim.*
[314] *NE*, pp. 252, 253, 257; *NKH*, pp. 90, 93*NBE*, p. 297.
[315] *NV*, pp. 63–4, 66, 80.

A Troubled Background

Natural Disasters

Cistercian monastic communities suffered many dfficulties. Individual monks might suffer from *accidents*, such as Dominic Schnabel of Lilienfeld (A; *ob.* 1632), who 'in falling off his horse broke his neck and died seven hours later'. The necrologies also tell of such happenings to the laity, that of Bronnbach recording of one Christopher (*ob.* 1577) that 'he was trampled to death by a wild horse', whilst the obituary of Wilhering (A) informs us of Wienne de Shawnberg (*ob.* 1483), a local reeve or provost, 'who was thrown off his horse whilst riding vigorously and, alas, died'.[316]

Cistercians lived mostly by rivers or lakes, and several necrologies record monks and laity who were *drowned*, though the exact circumstances are not told. Neuencamp (G) had a monk, John, 'who drowned in the lake'. Pelplin (P) had a monk, still a deacon, Stanislaus (*ob.* 1592), who died in the river Vistula. Wilhering had a scribe, Laurence Hohenerler (*ob.* 1475), 'who drowned in the Danube near the stone which is called Wersenstein'. Valentine Janikowki, aged forty-six, of Szczyrzycz (P), drowned in 1788.[317]

---

[316] *NL*, p. 35; *NBR*, p. 107; *NW*, p. 112.
[317] *NN*, p. 517; *NPL*, p. 69; *NW*, p. 97; *NKN*, p. 95.

The necrology of Wettingen (Sw) records the death of Count Hartmann of Hapsburg (*ob.* 1281), who drowned in the Rhine. It also relates a sad tale of events on 24 October 1433: 'At the hour of vespers a boat was in peril near the monastery [presumably on the river Limmat]; six men and women drowned, and lie buried in our cemetery'. Worse still! The record further relates that in 1462 'Abbot John Wagner of Wettingen with his notary, Martin Barhamer, and local people, men and women, in all numbering sixty persons, were making their way to Basle [obviously by river], but all drowned in the Rhine'; perhaps the boat was overloaded?[318]

Several necrologies make mention of *infectious diseases*, plagues, generally referred to as *peste* or 'pestilence'. As the Black Death spread through Europe we learn that in 1348 nineteen members of the community of Zwettl (A) died, whilst La Cour-Dieu (F) lost seventeen monks, four novices and four *conversi*. The obituary of Kaisheim (G) recorded that 'here we have in memory fourteen monks, two novices and six *conversi*, whose names are known to God, who died in the year 1350 within one month from 27 March, the feast of Easter, to 17 April'.[319]

'Morbid pestilence' in 1463 affected Fürstenfeld (G), and in 1483 Fürstenzell (G). The obituary of Raitenhaslach (G) states that when plague hit the nunnery of Selingenthal (Landshut, G) in 1495, the

---

[318] *NWT*, pp. 598, 596, 595.
[319] *NZ*, p. 573; *NCD*, p. 180; *NKH*, p. 90.

A Troubled Background

abbess, four nuns and four child scholars died. The appendix to Seligenthal's own obituary tells us that Abbess Barbara Gumpenpergerin, sixteen religious and eight girl scholars all perished. Seven monks of Neuberg (A) died of plague in 1541, as did Simon Loizewicz, the cellarer of Pelplin (P), in 1564. The keeping of the *obits* at Rein (A) on 11 September of an abbot and eleven monks may imply deaths from plague.[320]

Disease saw the deaths of two *conversi* of Oliwa (P) in 1602, and at Ląd (P) in 1630. Plague affected the Jędrzejów region of Poland in the autumn of 1623; one *conversus* and several of those in fraternity with the abbey died. Plague affected Koronowo (P) in the summer months of 1630, when nine of its religious died, and Oliwa suffered again in 1653, with three novices affected, one of whom died.[321] At an unknown date at Königsbronn (G), 'John, Ulrich, Conrad, monks, and many others' died. When, in 1611, severe plague threatened Salem (A), the monks turned to fasting, and the offering of a solemn Mass to Our Lady in her chapel.[322]

A damaging natural occurrence might be that of *fire*. The necrology of Kamieniec (P) tells how 'at the time of Matins' (i.e. in the night), 'lightning struck and set fire to the monastery'. At an unknown date,

---

[320] *NF*, p. 122–3; *NR*, p. 275; *NSA*, p. 512; *NNB*, p. 34; *NPL*, p. 104; *NRE*, p. 350.
[321] *NOL*, pp. 523–4; *NLA*, pp. 496–7; *NOL2*, pp. 2–3; *NJD*, pp. 793–7; *NKN*, p. 9.
[322] *NR*, p. 274; *NSL*, pp. 360–1.

John le Ponte, archdeacon of Autun, gave Preuilly (F) fifty Tours pounds to defray its costs 'for reparation after an unexpected fire set alight both its refectory and dormitory'. At Pairis (F) Henry Toritz (*ob.* 1504), prior for twenty-five years, was lauded for his work in restoration after a fire there. Severe fires also affected Jędrzejów around 1726 (when the monastery was 'consumed by fire'), and in 1799 (with a 'conflagration of monastery and church').[323]

War and Conflict

The early thirteenth century[324] in north-eastern Poland, under pagan Prussian dominance, was unsettling for the Cistercians there. The necrology of Oliwa records that in 1234 (perhaps an error for 1224), the monastery was burnt by the Prussians, and six *conversi* were killed; 'the community was led to Gdańsk by the Prussians', and the third abbot, Ethler, 'was credited with martyrdom'. Three other *conversi* and a monk were killed, in different locations away from the monastery, and one monk was imprisoned. In 1577 an uprising by the people of Gdańsk saw the monastery again destroyed, and the sub-prior, Paul Lang, lost his life.[325]

---

[323] *NKM*, image 1; *NP*, p. 887; *NPS*, p. 82; pp. 794–6.
[324] The dates are hard to determine, but the third abbot of Tennenbach (1158), Conrad, was caught up in fighting, and died during a civil war: *NT*, p. 342.
[325] *NOL*, pp. 504, 508, 515, 518, 530–4. Abbot of Oliwa, Casimir Ethler, was killed by the Prussians on 27 September 1224: W. Kętrzyński, 'Series Abbatum Olivensis', in *MPH* IV,

A Troubled Background

Attacks on individual monks and *conversi* were to continue. The necrology of Kołbacz (P) told of 10 August 1329, that 'On this day two priest monks, Arnold of Repin and John of Stargen, were captured by a certain apostate *conversus* of our house, Willekin by name, living in Ukervelde, at Prilop Grange, who placed them in strong bonds, and on the morrow of Saint Laurence [11th August] they suffered together an execrable death, namely hung in a pillory'. The obituary of Salem (A) records how in August 1362, two *conversi*, John Kupar and Berthold, were killed away from the monastery by Count Godfrid Wartenstein and his accomplices, and that in 1496, another *conversus*, Peter Wagner, was 'killed by the sword near the kitchen of the peasantry'.[326]

Other religious to be murdered included a monk, Erhard Fyrczing, 'killed by the sword near the washing-place' in 1426, when the Hussites burnt Zwettl abbey (A). In 1429 Abbot Peter I of Neuzelle, and others of its monks, died with their hands and feet cut off by the Hussites. They were seen as martyrs. Abbot Nicholas II of Neuzell (*ob.* 1469) restored the monastery after its devastation by the Hussites.[327]

Attacks might take place on religious and servants caring for an abbey's possessions, such as Nicholas Punnocius (*ob.* 1592), 'faithful servant of Pelplin (P), speared through while defending our property

---

Lwów, 1884, p. 137.
[326] *NK*, p. 495; *NSL*, pp. 221, 24.
[327] *NZ*, p. 576; *NNC*, n.p.

at Pogokau', and a monk, Edmund Lewandowski (*ob.* 1710), 'killed on the public way' whilst defending property of Ląd (P). The necrologies are full of references to others killed. The *obit* of a monk of Cambron (B), Matthew de Lobes (*ob.* 1332), noted that 'He saw a Jew wounded in the open at the Virgin of Cambron'.[328]

The Sixteenth Century

The Reformation and the spread of militant Lutheranism affected a number of monasteries in central and western Europe, and severe problems also came with the expansion of the Ottoman Empire under Suleiman the Magnificent. The Hungarian abbey of Pilis was destroyed by the Turks on 7 September 1526, and a later necrology noted a 'memorial on this day of the monks and priests of Pilis who were burnt'. In fact, one monk was killed, and all those who could took refuge at the monastery of Heiligenkreuz (A), but it also suffered in 1536. At Heilgenkreuz in 1527 George, one of the refugee monks, died, and later, in 1541, the last abbot of Pilis, John Norman. The monastery of Paszto (Hg) was 'devastated by the Turks' in 1544; some monks were slaughtered, others took refuge at Heiligenkreuz; the last abbot, Luke II, of Paszto, died there in 1568. A century later, Martin Llifalus, first abbot of Zirc (Hg), was captured and killed by the Turks, whilst

---

[328] *NPL*, p. 66; *NLA*, p. 475; *NC*, p. 127.

A Troubled Background

in 1683 a monk of Heiligenkreuz, Wolfgang Silber, was cruelly killed when the Turks blew up a property of the abbey.[329]

An uprising by the local, now Lutheran, peasantry in 1525 meant that the abbot of Ebrach (G) fled to Nuremberg. Alas! He wore his monastic habit; though he went 'in hope of evasion', it was seen by the locals as 'peculiar and ridiculous', and he was seized. His monastery was ransacked and burnt, the damage amounting to 200,000 florins, but a decade later the burnt choir stalls and sedilia had been restored. In that same year of 1525, a similar uprising by the peasantry did much damage to Lucelle abbey (F) and its neighbourhood, including monuments in the abbey church. It was a year when the Zwinglian movement rose to a peak, and anti-Roman feeling was everywhere.[330]

In 1537 the monks of Maulbronn were forced by the Lutheran tide to move for safety to their paired abbey of Pairis. John of Lenzingen, abbot of Maulbronn and Pairis (*ob.* 1547), was noted as 'a man of sound instruction, and of admirable forbearance, as he bore for the Catholic faith numerous persecutions and attacks'. He may have been succeeded by Henry Reutter, of whom the necrology says that he was 'after the introduction of heresy at Maulbronn, last abbot there, and at Pairis'. To Pairis came also,

---

[329] *NHG, passim, NNC*, n.p.; Cf. Ferenc L. Hervay, *Repertorium Historicum Ordinis Cisterciensis in Hungaria*, Rome, 1984, pp. 129, 132, 145.

[330] *NEBR*, p. 209; *NLC*, p. 44.

with some monks, Leonard Jos (*ob.* 1562), prior of Bebenhausen (G), expelled by the duke of Württemberg, Ulrich I (*ob.* 1550), when he introduced the Reformation in his land. Leonard became prior of Pairis and was buried in the choir. Abbot Nicholas of Maulbronn (*ob.* 1557) was said to be a 'defender of the Catholic faith'. Several of the monks of Bebenhausen, however, adopted the evangelical cause in 1534.[331]

Boneffe (F) was 'burnt by heretics' in 1568, and a *conversus*, Peter Lampe, forester, was hung and killed. The destruction meant that a familiar, Peter van der Gheheucht, had to be buried in the secular cemetery. When the abbey was burnt in 1578, the monks of Baudeloo (B) took refuge first in Cologne, where one, Baldwin Valle (*ob.* 1581), died, then from 1590 in Gand (Ghent), where Cistercian nuns lived at Bijloke. Their convent was sacked in 1579, but they were able to return to it in 1585.

It appears that some of the monks of Baudeloo were dispersed, taking on parochial duties, whilst three abbots were referred to as 'external abbots', as they could no longer live in their abbey, nor be buried at their house; indeed, they died 'in Benedictine habit'. Prior Anthony Churnis (*ob.* 1582) was buried at Himmerod abbey (G). This was the consequence of the establishment of the Calvinistic Ghent Republic (1577–84). The necrology of Baudeloo tells us of the death in 1597 of Charles D'Hooghe, the first

---

[331] *NPS*, pp. 79–80, 82; *NNC*, n.p., *NBE*, pp. 291–8.

A Troubled Background

monk to die 'since the return', and by 1616 a new abbey church had been built in Ghent.[332]

The Seventeenth Century

Several Cistercian monasteries were affected by the Thirty Years' War, and by the growth of the Swedish Empire, following the accession of Gustav Adolph to the Swedish throne in 1611. Some were closed, and their religious had to seek refuge elsewhere. Pelplin (P), not far inland from the Baltic coast, was to suffer, and one of its monks, Blaise, died at Obra (P) abbey in 1627, 'at the time of our dispersion', and another, John Poleus (*ob.* 1630), at the convent of Marienstern (G), where he heard confessions. However, Stanislaus Budziński, Gaspar Kuraz, Andrew Skowron and John Sleszynski, lay-folk, all of whom died in 1627 'in skirmishes with the Swedes', left Pelplin between them a total of 1,580 florins.[333]

A monk of Langheim (G), Benedict Arnold (*ob.* 1633), died in exile 'on account of the Swedish wars', which also caused Abbot John Feiltzer of Bronnbach (G; *ob.* 1637), to spend four years away from his monastery. Abbot Seraphim Heitschmann of Maulbronn (G) went into exile at Loccum abbey in Saxony. Christmann Ruppus, prior of Pairis, also lost his life in 1636 on account of the Swedish wars, as did a monk of Koronowo (P) in 1650, three others

---

[332] *NBN*, pp. 264, 291 *NB*, ff. 9v, 20r–v, 21v, 22r, and *passim*.
[333] *NPL*, pp. 70, 93, 101.

in 1664, and two more at unknown dates.[334] At this period the Thirty Years' War saw Abbot Hugh Stimmer of Neuzelle (G) expelled from his monastery; dying in 1632 he was buried at Krzeszów abbey, now in Poland, then in Lower Silesia.[335]

The community of Salem (A), 'by unanimous consent' and 'on account of the raging wars of the times', placed their monastery in 1675 under the patronage of St Joseph. Fire destroyed its church in 1697, but the abbacy of Stephen Jung (*ob.* 1725), the thirty-fifth abbot, saw 'the new building of this monastery constructed after the burning of the monastery in the wars of the times'. Lutheranism was to the fore: in September 1689, Joseph Coulond, a *conversus* of Aulps, was 'killed under the bridge by the prison by heretics from the valley of Lucerne'.[336]

In northern France the year 1661 saw very many Huguenots fleeing to England, but at this time the abbey of Notre-Dame-des-Champs (F) was suspected of Jansenist leanings, and frowned upon. This explains the entry in its necrology praising its Sister Catherine. Born in 1636, the daughter of a famous painter, Philip of Champagne, and a pupil of the nunnery from the age of twelve-and-a-half years, she took the habit in 1656, and was professed the next year. 'She chose to share the misery which enveloped

---

[334] *NLH*, p. 289; *NLC*, pp. 31–232; *NPS*, p. 74; *NKN*, pp. 11, 15–16.
[335] *NNC*, n.p., Benedict Arnold died at 'Albi Moenii', not yet traced.
[336] *NSL*, pp. 75, 108; *NAP*, p. 136.

the community in the times of persecution which started in 1661'. By this time she had lost the use of her legs, became worse and suffered from 'high fever', gave herself to intense prayer, and later in life had a miraculous cure, 'following which she could descend a stair-case of forty steps', which tells something of the interior architecture of the abbey.[337]

In Belgium the monastery of St-Bernard-sur-l'Escaut for a time lost its independence to the bishopric of Antwerp, that prelate perhaps having been made its commendatory abbot. Freedom was to come, and when Judoci Gillis died in 1660, it was noted that he was 'the twenty-ninth abbot, and the first since the separation from the bishopric of Antwerp'.[338]

The Eighteenth to Nineteenth Centuries

The reign of Joseph II as Holy Roman Emperor (1763–90) saw about one-third of all religious houses in his kingdom suppressed, the necrology of Neuzelle telling of the deposition from his office suffered by Abbot Reiner II of Zwettl (A; *ob.* 1810).[339]

At the end of the eighteenth century the French Revolution meant the closure in January 1797 of the nunnery at Soleilmont (B) for some six and a half years. During this short exile the obituary of the convent tells us of the death of Philip Stephen Joseph Drion, who made available, free of charge, his cha-

---

[337] *NPRL2*, pp. 467–8.
[338] *NBM*, p. 31; cf. p. 14.
[339] *NC*, n.p.

teau at Farciennes, where the sisters lived until their return home. In November 1797 one of the exiled sisters, a jubilarian, Ursula Monte, died, and was buried at Epp-Sauvage. The following year another jubilarian, Rose Longpré, passed away 'in the midst of our sisters', and was laid to rest at Farciennes. The necrology also notes that the sisters returned to Soleilmont in 1802.[340]

The French Revolution also brought about the closure of Villers (B) in 1796. Western Belgium had formed part of the Austrian Empire, and William Chantinnes, provisor of the monastery, was caught up in 1789 in the conflicts between the Belgians and the 'Austrian tyrants'. Held captive in Namur, he manged to escape and return to the abbey. On taking office in 1788 the sixty-fourth abbot of Villers faced similar difficulties. He took shelter in a refuge of Aulne abbey for four months, and then with 'the noble nuns of Hocht' (B). The Napoleonic Wars against the Austro-Hungarian Empire led to the death in 1809 in Slovakia of Bernard Hromadka, monk of Vyšší Brod, and an army chaplain.[341]

Salem was suppressed in 1802 and its monks displaced. Its necrology lists a dozen of its monks who died beween 1804 and 1818. The first monk to die since the abbey's closure was Marian Sillmann (*ob.* 1804), who was buried near Salem in the 'common cemetery at Stephansfelden'; in 1814 it was also

---

[340] *NSO*, pp. 413, 417, 434.
[341] *NV*, pp. 83, 86; *NNC*, n.p.

A Troubled Background

the resting-place of another monk, John Augustan, previously organist and music professor in the monastery.[342] Basil Miller, professor of Rhetoric at Salem (*ob.* 1814), became parish priest of Hilzingen, and was buried there, and Jerome Muchet, monk (*ob.* 1818), now priest of Weildorf, was interred there. A former *conversus* and wool worker, Zacharias Hanflig, who became became mentally ill, and later died, was buried in his native village of Pforzheim.[343]

The closure of Neuberg (A) in 1786 meant that two monks, Kosmas Werber (*ob.* 1812) and Joseph Berger (*ob.* 1840), were both buried in Graz. Hauterive being suppressed in 1848, the former prior, Benedict Merlet, moved to Arconciel, and was interred there. Abbot Robert Magnin died, aged seventy-three, at his family home in Vuippens. Laurence Schorro, monk, died at Marly aged sixty-three in 1871, where he had moved 'after the unjust suppression of the monastery', and Albert, monk (*ob.* 1857), a native of Fribourg, moved back there, and in 1857, aged fifty-two, was buried there 'in the common cemetery'.[344]

The Twentieth Century

The necrology of Neuzelle tells of the difficulties Cistercians have suffered from the Nazis and the Communists. Those who suffered in the Second World War included Englebert Blœchl, monk of Vyšší

---

[342] *NSL, passim,* and pp. 247–9.
[343] *NSL,* pp. 166, 72, 135.
[344] *NNB,* p. 44; *NHR,* pp. 49–50, 56, 105.

Brod (C), burnt in 1942 at Dachau. In 1941 Bernard Burgstaller of Wilhering (A) was 'imprisoned by the Nazis, cruelly maltreated, and died miserably in a prison near Krefeld'; he was buried at Wilhering. Others killed in the war included Henry Wagner (1941; cleric at Vyšší Brod), Norbert Staudinger (1942; *conversus* of Vyšší Brod, and 'a good example of a lay-brother') and Laurence Schwarzbauer (1945; *conversus* of Heiligenkreuz, A).[345]

Abbot Martin II of Lilienfeld (*ob*. 1958) was a military chaplain, who 'after the Great War restored the monastery; musical, and a clear singer'. Abbot Eberhard Harzer, expelled with his monks from Osek by the Communists in 1949, re-edified Raitenhaslach. Abbot Tecelin Iaksch (*ob*. 1954) of Vyšší Brod on expulsion moved with his monks to Rein (A). Abbot Cassian Haid, abbot of Mehrerau and abbot-general, was forced by the National Socialist Movement to leave for Hauterive abbey (Sw), which he rescusitated, but he was later able to return home. Albert Siwek (*ob*. 2008), abbot emeritus of Wąchock (P), expelled by the Communists, became adminstrator at Vyšší Brod (C).[346] These are, of course, but a few of the disturbances religious orders faced in the post-war years.

---

[345] *NNC*, n.p.
[346] *NNC*, n.p.

CONCLUSION

I hope this essay has demonstrated that a study of Cistercian necrologies can very much amplify the information afforded by monastic chronicles, and other manuscript material. Monastic necrologies portray not only monastic history, but also the everyday life of their times, and events that occurred outside a monastery's precinct wall. By their very nature, necrologies often strike a sombre note, but my study can conclude with a very positive outlook, for when Ebrach monastery was suppressed in 1803, its obituary tells us that its abbot was given a pension of 8,000 Rhine florins, each priest professed for at least ten years received 600 florins; those under ten years, 500 florins; clerical brothers, 400 florins; senior *conversi* 350 florins; junior *conversi*, 300 florins.[347] Nothing happened on that scale at the late medieval dissolution of religious life in my native Wales!

---

[347] *NEBR*, pp. 324–5.

Lightning Source UK Ltd.
Milton Keynes UK
UKHW041144300322
400832UK00003B/37